# The Carbohydrate Craver's Diet Cookbook

# THE Carbohydrate Craver's DIET COOKBOOK

**Judith J. Wurtman, Ph.D.,
and Margaret Leibenstein**

HOUGHTON MIFFLIN COMPANY • BOSTON
1984

**Library of Congress Cataloging in Publication Data**

Wurtman, Judith J.
The carbohydrate craver's diet cookbook.

Includes index.
1. Low-calorie diet.   2. High-carbohydrate diet.
3. Low-calorie diet—Recipes.   4. High-carbohydrate
diet—Recipes.   I. Leibenstein, Margaret.   II. Title.
RM222.2.W873      1984      613.2′5      83-18470
ISBN 0-395-35424-2

Printed in the United States of America

s 10 9 8 7 6 5 4 3 2 1

# Acknowledgments

There are several people without whose amazing efforts this book would never have seen the light of day, and we wish to thank them.

First, thanks to Frances Tenenbaum, who originally suggested writing this book. She is our editor, friend, and taster *par excellence.* Her direction, organization, gentle prodding, and gentler criticism made possible what, at times, we believed to be an impossibility — the completion of this book.

Thanks also to Helen Rees, our friend, confidante, and agent, for her patience and persistence on our behalf.

Finally, to the staff at Houghton Mifflin we owe a very special debt of gratitude. They performed their jobs in a period of time hitherto reserved for the wand wavings of the Wizard of Oz, yet they were always pleasant, helpful, remarkably cheerful, and, it goes without saying, competent. We thank you all.

Judith Wurtman and
Margaret Leibenstein

*The Carbohydrate Craver's Diet Cookbook* was written because of the enthusiasm of my husband Richard and my children, Rachael and David, for this project. They inevitably met my hesitations about writing this book with assurances that long lines of their friends were waiting, cooking spoon in hand, for our recipes.

v

This book was helped along to its completion by positive responses from many of my patients to the recipes I shared with them. Their desire to obtain the book certainly spurred my efforts to see it finished as soon as possible.

My ability to work on the cookbook was helped immeasurably by the unfailing willingness of my MIT co-worker Sharon Mark, who took on many of our mutual research obligations, especially when deadlines threatened. I am extremely grateful to her inevitable "I'll do it" response when research and writing commitments conflicted.

The best part of writing the book has been my friendship with its co-author. Marge's incredible wit, imagination, and good humor have made working on this book a total delight. Our only disagreement was over the naming of a particular kasha dish (I thought my grandmother might have objected) and the only problem we had in working together was that constant laughter interfered with the "seriousness" of the writing.

J.W.

Writing a cookbook is never a solitary act. Obviously, without the efforts of Judith Wurtman and her colleagues at MIT there would be no Carbohydrate Craver's Diet and therefore no *Carbohydrate Craver's Diet Cookbook.* My collaboration with Judy, which originated out of mutual need, grew into friendship and then real affection. It has been a delight working with her.

In developing the recipes I leaned heavily on past experiences and am therefore indebted to my teachers, my students, and my dinner guests for all they've taught me about cooking. In addition, a conversation with Adriane Ruderman of Boston resulted in Adriane's Dressing; Dr. and Mrs. Veniero Marsan of Rome, Italy, and Professor and Mrs. Franco Romani of the University of Rome not only contributed ideas for the section on pasta but greatly facilitated my work during my stay in their beautiful city; friends and colleagues in the Women's Culinary Guild were a great source of support, suggestions, and information. I am grateful to both Margaret Northrup and Mary Bosco, who interrupted very busy schedules to provide help with typing at critical periods in the preparation of the manuscript.

Proofreading a cookbook requires very special knowledge and dedication. Elizabeth Bishop caught errors and omissions with the practiced eye of the true culinary professional that she is, and displayed the expertise that has made her so useful to Julia Child and other great cooks with whom she has worked.

However, no degree of diligence or effort can ensure a perfect manuscript. Any dissatisfaction with the recipes, or errors that may have gone undetected, must be laid at my doorstep and mine alone.

Finally, my husband Harvey Leibenstein has been unfailingly supportive in the face of temper tantrums, self-doubt, repetitive meals (*"We'll eat this mess until I get it right!"*), and innumerable other discomforts that I afforded him in preparing this book. His delightful sense of humor never failed him or me and for this I love and thank him.

M.L.

*For my husband and children*
J.W.


*For Frieda, Samuel, and Harold Libnic*
*and for Harvey*
M.L.

# *Contents*

# PART I

## The Carbohydrate Craver's Diet

# 1

## *The Carbohydrate Connection*

The Carbohydrate Craver's Diet is a weight-loss plan for the dieter who craves sweet and starchy foods. The diet grew out of our research into the brain chemistry of carbohydrate hunger at the Massachusetts Institute of Technology. We found that all people and animals have a specific appetite for carbohydrate foods: starchy foods like bread, potatoes, pasta, rice, and cereals and sweet foods like pastries, candy, fruit, and ice cream. The carbohydrate hunger is turned on and off by the brain chemical serotonin. Some of us — the Carbohydrate Cravers — have an urge to eat these foods both at meals and as an afternoon or evening snack.

We also discovered why Carbohydrate Cravers fail to lose weight permanently on any of the popular low-carbohydrate diets. After a few weeks, or even days, of being forbidden carbohydrates, the brain loses its ability to turn off carbohydrate hunger when you return to eating normal amounts of sweet or starchy foods. That is why you find yourself polishing off a box of crackers or cookies when you normally would be satisfied with only a few.

You probably think that you can't control your carbohydrate appetite because you have no will power. You are wrong. You have *will* power, but you don't have the *brain* power to stop overeating carbohydrates. The low-carbohydrate programs that seduce many dieters prevent the sero-

3

tonin in your brain from signaling you to stop soon enough.

The only way you can *lose* weight and *gain* control over your carbohydrate appetite is to follow the Carbohydrate Craver's Diet. (See the Appendix for an explanation of the scientific basis of the Carbohydrate Craver's Diet.)

## The Diet

On the Carbohydrate Craver's Diet, you — or the carbohydrate-craving dieter in your family — eat 1100 calories a day — 900 calories at meals, plus a 200-calorie snack. The number of grams of carbohydrates you must eat as the snack was determined by our research findings and is the amount we found will turn off your carbohydrate hunger.

The diet plan includes all the vitamins, minerals, and protein everyone requires for good health. You can continue this program as long as necessary because it is nutritionally balanced.

The average person can expect to lose about 10 pounds a month on the Carbohydrate Craver's Diet. Obviously, the number of pounds you have to lose and the type and amount of exercise you do influence the rate of loss. Those who must shed great amounts of weight usually lose even faster.

## The Menu Plans

We think you'll find the Carbohydrate Craver's Diet the easiest one you've ever tried. You will be eating the foods you enjoy, and you won't have to count calories or juggle "exchange lists." Furthermore, because the daily menus provide all the calories, carbohydrates, protein, fat, vitamins, and minerals you need every day, you may choose *any* day's menu whenever and as often as you like. There is no established order — just follow your own preferences.

Each day's menu is built around a main-course recipe — usually a one-dish meal. If you want pasta for dinner, for example, choose a pasta recipe; the facing page spells out the menu you should follow that day. You must use the menu that accompanies each recipe because we have incorporated the main course into a food plan for the entire day to make sure you consume the correct amounts of calories and nutrients.

Suppose you don't like the breakfast or the lunch on that day's menu. No problem. Chapter 3 lists four Basic Breakfasts and four Basic Lunches that you may substitute for the breakfast and lunch on the day's food plan. Below each recommended breakfast and lunch, you will find the number of the Basic Breakfast or Lunch to use as the substitute. The substitute breakfasts and lunches contain the same nutrients as the ones they replace on the daily menu plans.

In addition to the foods listed on the daily menus, you may drink as much tea, coffee, or noncaloric soft beverages as you like. But don't substitute these beverages for any of those on the menu. If you don't want to drink the called-for milk or fruit juice at mealtime, drink it between meals.

Weigh and measure your food during the first few weeks on the diet to be sure that your portions contain the recommended amounts. Dust off the cobwebs from your old food scale or buy a new one and put it in a convenient place, along with measuring cups and spoons. Once you are sure of the correct sizes and weights, weigh only when you think it necessary. (Don't worry about getting the correct amounts of vegetables or fruit. We have allowed for variances in produce size.)

The 200-calorie snack is an essential part of the plan. You *must* eat the entire amount every day at your peak craving time.

## *The Super Salads*

Most of the daily menus include a serving of Super Salad, which is sometimes split between lunch and dinner. The recipes for these low-calorie, high-vitamin salads, with recipes for delicious, easily prepared low-calorie salad dressings, appear in Chapter 4. On days when Super Salads are not on the menu, your vitamins are supplied in other foods.

## The Recipes

The science of carbohydrate hunger makes the diet work — but these recipes make the diet a delight. They use many favorite foods — pastas, rice, potatoes, breads, and bean and grain dishes — imaginatively, but they are easy to prepare and add taste and pleasure to your diet. These delicious, low-calorie entrées supply the high-fiber, low-fat foods that the surgeon general and others recommend for *everybody*, whether or not they are dieting.

If you are feeding a family, you will find that all the members will enjoy this diet. The size of the dieter's serving is determined by the menu, but the rest of the family can eat as much as they want of these dishes — even the larger portions are relatively low in calories, extremely nutritious, and inexpensive. The four- or six-serving recipes are most suitable for family meals, but many can be halved or doubled. And since these dishes taste just as good or better the next day, you can cook for more than one day at a time. Many of these foods freeze well; we suggest dividing them into diet-sized portions (especially if you cook only for yourself) to have a good supply of meals available in the freezer.

## Special Diet Needs

People who have food allergies or aversions may find it difficult to follow some of the meal plans. An allergy to milk, that is, lactose intolerance, may be alleviated by adding to the milk a preparation that predigests the lactose. Consult your doctor for its applicability and name. Lactose-intolerant people can often tolerate cheese or other dairy products, so substitute these foods for milk on the menu plans. If you cannot eat any dairy products, ask your doctor to recommend a calcium supplement to provide that major nutrient of dairy products. And increase the amount of protein in the dinner recipe by 1 ounce to compensate for the protein supplied by the dairy products.

Green peppers, strawberries, cabbage, parsley, and citrus fruits are all high in vitamin C. If you are allergic to one of them, substitute another. Ask your doctor whether you should have a vitamin C supplement if you can't tolerate any of these foods.

The menu plan is nutritionally complete. However, if you usually take a vitamin-mineral supplement or eat a fortified breakfast cereal, feel free to continue. Menstruating women should consider taking an iron supplement, since iron is relatively scarce in the food supply except in red meat or shellfish.

People who must maintain a salt-restricted diet may wish to shun recipes that include bouillon, canned soups, and other canned foods. Salt-free substitutes may be used.

# 2

## *The Snacks*

The basis of the Carbohydrate Craver's Diet is the carbohydrate snack. You must eat a sweet or starchy snack every day when you feel hungriest for a carbohydrate food. Don't worry about the calories because they have been included in the diet total of 1100 per day.

Choose a snack from the list in this chapter. They all contain the correct numbers of calories and grams of carbohydrates appropriate to the Carbohydrate Craver's Diet plan.

If you are not sure of the exact time your peak craving period occurs, keep track for a few days of the time your carbohydrate hunger is sharpest. You can recognize it easily because even when your stomach may be full, you still have a yen to eat "something." You feel out of sorts, restless, perhaps a little tense or grumpy, and think to yourself, "I really must eat something sweet or starchy." The time that feeling is strongest is your carbohydrate-craving time.

If you have a strong carbohydrate hunger twice a day — perhaps around 3:00 or 4:00 in the afternoon and again around 8:00 or 9:00 at night — plan to snack twice a day. Although the pounds may come off a little more slowly, you will be able to stick to the diet for a long time because you will never be hungry for carbohydrates. All the weight you have to lose will come off eventually.

Don't eat your snack right after a meal. Eating the snack close to mealtime prevents it from satisfying your carbohydrate hunger. In order for your brain to recognize that you have just eaten a carbohydrate snack, you must eat it at least an hour and a half to two hours after a meal. Otherwise, your brain cannot distinguish the snack from the mealtime foods your stomach is digesting. That is why there are no desserts on this diet.

Be sure to enjoy your snack. Sit down, put up your feet, find something enjoyable to read or music to listen to, watch TV, or do whatever you like. Relax. Eat your snack leisurely and deliberately. Never, never gobble it as you race from one task to another. When you eat fast, you always eat too much.

Even though the snack list contains many products found in most parts of the country, not all supermarkets carry all of them. If you want to substitute a different snack for one on the list, check the calorie and carbohydrate content to make sure it contains no more than 220 calories and at least 25 to 30 grams of carbohydrate.

Some manufacturers change the package weights of their foods as the price of sugar fluctuates. Look at the label and compare the weight of your chosen snack with the weight of the comparable food on the snack list. If the weight varies by only half an ounce, you may eat the snack. The 30 to 40 additional calories won't affect your rate of weight loss. However, if the difference is much greater, find another snack.

Snack on the same food every day for at least two weeks at a time so you don't cater to your taste buds rather than your carbohydrate hunger. After a few days of eating the same snack, you will perceive that your body really craves the carbohydrate — not the taste — and that will be totally satisfying.

## Snacks by Carbohydrate Content

### STARCHY SNACKS

| Snack | Amount | Carbohydrate (grams) | Calories |
|---|---|---|---|
| Wasa Crisp Bread, Hearty Rye | 6 crackers | 66 | 192 |
| RyKrisp | 6 triple crackers | 54 | 180 |
| Wasa Crisp Bread, Sport | 5 crackers | 45 | 200 |
| Rice crackers, any flavor | 10 | 44 | 200 |
| Melba toast | 13 slices | 43 | 199 |
| Mister Salty Veri-Thin pretzel sticks (Nabisco) | 2 ounces | 42 | 200 |
| Mister Salty Veri-Thin pretzels (Nabisco), 3-ring variety | 18 small | 41 | 198 |
| English muffin (Thomas' or Wonder), plus 1 tablespoon nondiet jelly | 1 | 41 | 183 |
| Wasa Crisp Bread, Golden Rye | 5 crackers | 40 | 195 |
| Ideal Flatbread | 5 crackers | 40 | 170 |
| Rice cakes (25 calories each) | 8 | 40 | 200 |
| Rice cakes (36 calories each) | 5 | 38 | 180 |
| Popcorn, no butter | 3½ cups | 37 | 189 |
| Matzo, plus 1 tablespoon nondiet jelly | 1 | 37 | 167 |
| Graham crackers | 7 single | 37 | 167 |
| Egg Jumbo (Stella D'oro) | 4 | 36.5 | 176 |
| Corn muffin, average size, with 1 tablespoon nondiet jelly | 1 | 36 | 191 |
| Blueberry muffin rounds, frozen (Morton), with 1 tablespoon nondiet jelly | 1 | 36 | 160 |

| Snack | Amount | Carbohydrate (grams) | Calories |
|---|---|---|---|
| Barnum's Animal Crackers (Nabisco) | 17 | 33 | 200 |
| Zwieback | 6 | 32 | 192 |
| Bran muffin, average size, with 1 tablespoon nondiet jelly | 1 | 32 | 154 |
| Saltines | 14 | 32 | 196 |
| Uneeda Biscuits | 9 | 32 | 189 |
| Butter Thins Crackers | 11 | 31 | 198 |
| Soda Crackers (Sunshine) | 10 | 30 | 200 |
| Bagel, average size, with 1 tablespoon diet margarine | 1 | 30 | 200 |
| Wheat Thins (Nabisco) | 22 | 27 | 198 |
| Bread sticks, sesame (Stella D'oro) | 4 | 27 | 212 |
| Waverly Thins | 11 | 27 | 198 |
| Chocolate Grahams (Nabisco) | 3 | 27 | 208 |
| French fried potatoes | 2 ounces | 26 | 187 |
| Bread sticks, plain (Stella D'oro) | 4 | 26 | 164 |
| Cheese Nips Crackers (Nabisco) | 38 | 25 | 200 |
| Better Cheddars Snack Thins (Nabisco) | 30 | 25 | 200 |

### SWEET SNACKS

| Snack | Amount | Carbohydrate (grams) | Calories |
|---|---|---|---|
| M & M's Plain Chocolate Candies | 1.4-ounce package | 55 | 201 |
| M & M's Royals Mint Chocolate | 1.26-ounce package | 55 | 182 |
| Butter Mints and Party Mints (Kraft) | 2 ounces | 51 | 208 |
| Marshmallows | 8 | 50 | 200 |

| Snack | Amount | Carbohydrate (grams) | Calories |
|---|---|---|---|
| Jelly beans | 30 (3 ounces) | 50 | 198 |
| Popsicle | 3 single | 50 | 195 |
| Pixy Stix (Sunline Brands) | 2 servings | 50 | 200 |
| Chuckles Jelly Candy (Nabisco) | 5 pieces (2-ounce package) | 50 | 200 |
| Gumdrops | 2 ounces | 49 | 198 |
| Popsicle, Kool-Pop | 8 | 48 | 192 |
| Popsicle, TwinPop | 2 bars | 47 | 190 |
| Fudgsicle | 2 | 47 | 204 |
| Spearmint Leaves (Brach) | 7 | 47 | 189 |
| Orange Slices (Brach) | 3 | 47 | 192 |
| Jelly Nougat (Brach) | 5 | 45 | 200 |
| Saltwater Taffy (Brach) | 5 | 44 | 200 |
| Big Ben Jellies (Brach) | 6 | 43 | 174 |
| Red Twist (Brach) | 2 ounces | 43 | 198 |
| Golden Fruit Raisin Biscuits (Sunshine) | 3 | 43 | 183 |
| Dixie Vanilla (Sunshine) | 3 | 43 | 180 |
| Fig Bars (Sunshine) | 4 | 41 | 180 |
| Orange and Perkys (Brach) | 3 | 41 | 165 |
| Wrapped Chocolates, Orange, Raspberry, Vanilla, Maple (Brach) | 3 | 41 | 192 |
| Chocolate Covered Mint Creme (Brach) | 3 | 41 | 195 |
| Licorice Twist (Brach) | 2 ounces | 40 | 186 |
| Good and Fruity | 1 package | 40 | 160 |
| Charleston Chew (Nabisco) | 1¾-ounce bar | 40 | 200 |
| Sherbet, orange | 6 ounces (¾ cup) | 40 | 180 |
| Bordeaux Cookies (Pepperidge Farm) | 8 | 40 | 192 |

| Snack | Amount | Carbohydrate (grams) | Calories |
|---|---|---|---|
| Aunt Sally Iced Cookies (Sunshine) | 2 | 40 | 198 |
| Frozen yogurt (Lite-line, Borden) | 7 ounces | 39 | 194 |
| Summit cookie bar | 1 package | 39 | 194 |
| Anisette Sponge (Stella D'oro) | 4 | 39 | 196 |
| Frozen yogurt (Strawberry Bar) | 3 bars | 38 | 207 |
| Milk Chocolate Covered Cherries (Brach) | 3 | 38 | 198 |
| Chocolate or Vanilla Treat (Weight Watchers) | 2 | 38 | 200 |
| Gingersnaps | 12 | 38 | 199 |
| Bit-O-Honey | 1 bar (1.7 ounces) | 38 | 188 |
| Good and Plenty | 1 package | 37 | 151 |
| MalloPuffs (Sunshine) | 3 | 37 | 199 |
| Molasses and Spice Cookies (Sunshine) | 3 | 36 | 201 |
| Lady Fingers | 4 large | 36 | 200 |
| Milkmaid Caramels (Brach) | 5 | 36 | 200 |
| Wrapped Chocolates, Cherry Nougat (Brach) | 3 | 35 | 174 |
| Caramels, plain or chocolate | 5 pieces (1½ ounces) | 35 | 188 |
| Chocolate Snaps (Sunshine) | 16 | 35 | 208 |
| Anisette Toast (Stella D'oro) | 4 | 35 | 172 |
| Pfeffernusse Spice Drops (Stella D'oro) | 5 | 34 | 180 |
| Iced Oatmeal Cookies (Sunshine) | 3 | 34 | 207 |
| Sprinkles (Sunshine) | 3 | 34 | 171 |

| Snack | Amount | Carbohydrate (grams) | Calories |
|---|---|---|---|
| Pop-Tarts (Kellogg), any flavor | 1 | 34 | 200 |
| Social Tea Biscuits (Nabisco) | 9 | 34 | 193 |
| Sugar Daddy Milk Caramel Pop | 1 lollipop (1⅜ ounces) | 33 | 185 |
| Sugared Egg Biscuits (Stella D'oro) | 3 | 33 | 192 |
| Assorted Royals (Brach) | 6 | 33 | 180 |
| Butter Thin Cookies (Rich) | 4 | 32 | 200 |
| Milky Way Snack Bar | 2 | 32 | 200 |
| Pudding Pops, frozen (Jell-O) | 2 | 32 | 200 |
| Ruffelo frozen ice-milk sandwich | 2 | 32 | 160 |
| Cream Lunch (Sunshine) | 4 | 32 | 180 |
| Brownie Nut Snack Bar (Pepperidge Farm) | 1 | 31 | 190 |
| Raisin Spice Snack Bar (Pepperidge Farm) | 1 | 31 | 170 |
| Breakfast Treats (Stella D'oro) | 2 | 31 | 210 |
| Piccolo Rolled Wafers (Nabisco) | 9 | 31 | 189 |
| Assorted Toffees (Brach) | 6 | 30 | 180 |
| Devil's Food Cupcake (Hostess) | 1 | 30 | 185 |
| Chocolate Sundae (Dairy Queen) | 1 small | 30 | 170 |
| Ice milk, vanilla, strawberry | 7 ounces | 29 | 190 |
| Date Nut Snack Bar (Pepperidge Farm) | 1 | 29 | 160 |
| Granola Clusters (Nature Valley), almond, caramel, raisin | 1 cluster | 28 | 150 |

| Snack | Amount | Carbohydrate (grams) | Calories |
| --- | --- | --- | --- |
| 3 Musketeers Snack Bar | 2 | 28 | 160 |
| Crumb cake, blueberry, cherry, French | 1 cake | 28 | 175 |
| Orbit Creme Sandwich (Sunshine) | 4 | 28 | 204 |
| Vanilla Wafers (Sunshine) | 13 | 28 | 195 |
| Hydrox (Sunshine), mint, vanilla, regular | 4 | 28 | 200 |
| Butter-Flavored Cookies (Sunshine) | 8 | 28 | 192 |
| Brown Edge Wafers (Nabisco) | 7 | 28 | 196 |
| Fig Pastry (Stella D'oro) | 2 | 28 | 190 |
| Ice-cream sandwich | 1 (2⅓ ounces) | 27 | 174 |
| Morning Light Donuts, frozen (Morton), chocolate iced, glazed, jelly | 1 | 26 | 200 |
| Sugar Wafers (Sunshine), plain or lemon | 4 | 26 | 176 |
| Oatmeal Cookies (Sunshine) | 3 | 26 | 174 |
| Apple Pastry (Stella D'oro) | 2 | 26 | 180 |
| Prune Pastry (Stella D'oro) | 2 | 26 | 180 |
| Bongos, frozen chocolate-covered pops (Thin's Inn) | 2 | 26 | 180 |

# 3

## Basic Breakfasts
## and Basic Lunches

The Carbohydrate Craver's Diet includes a 200-calorie breakfast, a 300-calorie lunch, and a 400-calorie dinner. In this cookbook, we have counted calories for you and developed a breakfast and a lunch menu to accompany each dinner recipe. By following the daily menu plan, you will get each day's quota of essential nutrients from the 900 calories consumed at meals.

If you don't like the breakfast or lunch that accompanies a particular menu, substitute one of the following four Basic Breakfasts or four Basic Lunches. They contain the same nutrients as the breakfast or lunch they replace. Below each breakfast and lunch menu, we give the number of the Basic Breakfast and Basic Lunch to substitute.

### Basic Breakfasts

**1**

½ cup orange *or* grapefruit juice
1 cup Bran Flakes *or* Cheerios
1 cup skim milk

**2**

½ cup orange juice
1 medium egg, boiled, or cooked in nonstick pan
1 slice whole wheat toast
1 tablespoon diet jelly

**3**

2 slices whole wheat toast
1 tablespoon diet jelly
1 tablespoon diet margarine
½ cup skim milk

**4**

½ cup orange *or* grapefruit juice
½ cup low-fat cottage cheese
1 1-ounce whole wheat bread pocket, toasted

## Basic Lunches

**1**

2 slices whole wheat bread
4 ounces lean cold cuts *or* 3 ounces water-packed
   tuna *or* 2½ ounces chicken
½ medium green pepper *or* ½ medium tomato
1 teaspoon diet mayonnaise *or* diet salad dressing
½ cup skim milk

**2**

1 cup low-fat cottage cheese
1 cup fresh or unsweetened frozen strawberries *or*
   cut-up orange, plus optional sweetener, *or*
   1 green pepper and 1 cucumber, cut up, plus optional seasonings
1 1-ounce whole wheat bread pocket *or* 3 rice cakes

## 3

1 slice whole wheat *or* rye bread
2 slices Lite-line cheese
½ serving any Super Salad
1 cup skim milk

## 4

1 bagel
1 ounce American, Swiss, Muenster, *or* Monterey
  Jack cheese
1 green pepper
1 carrot

*⊷§ Wake up hungry in the middle of the night? Keep some crackers and juice by your bed. If you eat them without leaving your bed, you'll be sleepy from eating the carbohydrate, warm from the bed, and fast asleep again soon.*

# 4

*Super Salads and Low-Calorie Dressings*

Most of the daily meal plans include a Super Salad, which is the nutritional foundation of the Carbohydrate Craver's Diet. It supplies your body's daily requirements of vitamins A and C and folic acid for a mere 75 to 80 calories a day. And this nutritional and caloric bargain saves you calories that you can "spend" on your snack.

The most important nutrient component of all the Super Salads is parsley, which is incorporated in three salad varieties: the Basic Super Salad, the Super Spinach Salad, and Super Coleslaw. The recipes for the salads and low-calorie salad dressings follow. (The calories in the salad dressings have been included with those for the salads, so feel free to add them in the quantities given. Or use commercially available low-calorie salad dressing.)

On some menu plans the amount of salad you eat is split equally between lunch and dinner; on others, the entire amount is eaten at a single meal. The reason is that the salads are tastier with some foods than with others. Some meal plans include only half a salad portion and some omit the salad because its ingredients are incorporated into one or more of the meals, or because the meals contain other fruits or vegetables that provide the same vitamins.

## *The Salads*

### BASIC SUPER SALAD

> 2 tablespoons chopped parsley
> ½ medium red or green pepper, cut up
> ½ cup shredded red *or* green cabbage
> 1 small carrot, chopped
> ½ cup scallions, onions, celery, *or* cucumber (optional)
> 1 cup alfalfa or bean sprouts (optional)
> 1 tablespoon diet salad dressing (optional)

### SUPER SPINACH SALAD

> 2 tablespoons chopped parsley
> 3½ ounces fresh spinach (½ cellophane bag)
> 4 large or 10 small fresh mushrooms, sliced
> 1 tablespoon soybean "bacon bits" (optional)
> 1 tablespoon diet salad dressing (optional)

### SUPER COLESLAW

> 2 tablespoons chopped parsley
> 1 cup shredded red *or* green cabbage
> 1 small carrot, chopped
> ½ cup scallions, onions, celery, *or* cucumber (optional)
> 2 tablespoons fresh dill *or* 1 teaspoon dried (optional)
> ½ dill pickle, chopped (optional)
> 1 tablespoon diet mayonnaise (optional)

## Low-Calorie Dressings

### FRENCH SEASONED-VINEGAR DRESSING

This basic recipe can be used either by itself or with added ingredients to dress all three Super Salads. You'll find it convenient to keep a supply of this seasoned vinegar around to use when you want a light, tart dressing. Be sure to store it in a tightly closed jar.

> 8 tablespoons red wine vinegar
> 4 tablespoons cold water
> 1½ teaspoons coarse salt
> ½ teaspoon Equal (low-calorie sweetener)
> 1 teaspoon freshly ground black pepper
> ½ teaspoon paprika
> ⅛ teaspoon dry mustard

Combine all the ingredients in a small, deep bowl and beat with a wire whisk until the salt and Equal are completely dissolved.

Pour into a screw-top jar and close tightly. Shake well before using.

> *Yield: approximately ¾ cup*
> *Calories per tablespoon: trace*

### GENOESE WINE VINEGAR

Use this dressing on a Salade Niçoise or a Super Salad, or sprinkle it on cold seafood. It adds the flavor of the famed Genoese pesto sauce without its calories.

> 3 cloves garlic, peeled and slightly bruised
> 3 sprigs fresh basil leaves
> 1 cup red wine vinegar
> ¾ cup water
> Pinch salt
> 1 drop almond extract

Thread the garlic cloves on a small wooden skewer if you have one, and insert them and the basil in a clean glass jar for which you have a tight-fitting cover. Set aside.

Combine the vinegar, water, salt, and extract in a small saucepan. Bring just to a boil and immediately remove from the heat.

Pour the hot vinegar mixture into the jar. Let it cool to room temperature and cover tightly.

Allow the vinegar mixture to steep for at least 48 hours before using. The longer you leave the garlic in the stronger its flavor becomes. If you prefer a light flavor, remove the garlic after 48 hours.

*Yield: approximately 1½ cups*
*Calories per tablespoon: trace*

## VINAIGRETTE DRESSING

Very nice over cooked asparagus or broccoli.

> ½ recipe French Seasoned-Vinegar Dressing (page 21), omit paprika
> 1 small stuffed green olive, chopped
> 1 teaspoon finely chopped capers
> 1 teaspoon finely chopped chives
> 1 teaspoon finely chopped parsley
> ½ tablespoon finely chopped dill pickle
> 1 hard-boiled egg yolk, finely chopped

Prepare the half recipe of French Seasoned-Vinegar Dressing (page 21). Combine the remaining ingredients, except the egg yolk, in a screw-top jar. Cover tightly and shake well.

Just before serving, add the chopped yolk and shake gently.

*Yield: 6 tablespoons*
*Calories per tablespoon: 10*

## PESTO-SEASONED VINEGAR DRESSING

This tasty variation on the basic Genoese Wine Vinegar is especially nice on salads that accompany pasta dishes.

½ recipe Genoese Wine Vinegar (p. 21)
¼ teaspoon paprika
Pinch dry mustard
¼ teaspoon Equal (low-calorie sweetener)
¼ teaspoon freshly ground black pepper
1 small clove garlic, bruised

Prepare the half recipe of Genoese Wine Vinegar. Combine the remaining ingredients in a screw-top jar, cover it tightly, and marinate overnight.

Discard the garlic before using the dressing.

*Yield: approximately ¾ cup*
*Calories per tablespoon: trace*

## SHERRY VINEGAR

½ cup dry sherry
1 cup cider vinegar
1 cup water
1 teaspoon honey

Combine all the ingredients in a medium saucepan. Bring the mixture just to a boil, reduce the heat immediately, and simmer 6 minutes.

Cool the mixture and store it in a very clean, tightly closed bottle or jar for at least 48 hours before using.

*Yield: approximately 2½ cups*
*Calories per tablespoon: 4*

&§ *Do you like to eat a big breakfast on weekends? Then skip lunch.*

## RASPBERRY VINEGAR

If you grow your own raspberries or can find wild ones or want to splurge and buy some in season, this is a wonderfully elegant vinegar to make in quantity. It livens up steamed vegetables and is excellent on cold pasta or rice salads.

2½ cups red wine vinegar
¾ cup water
1 teaspoon sugar
1 cup fresh ripe raspberries, in a clean 1-quart
    screw-top jar

Combine the vinegar, water, and sugar in a small saucepan. Stir until the sugar is dissolved.

Bring the mixture just to a boil. Pour it over the berries and cover the jar with a clean dish towel to absorb the moisture. Let it stand two hours until cool.

Close the jar tightly and store it in the refrigerator for at least 48 hours before using.

*Yield: approximately 2½ cups*
*Calories per tablespoon: 3*


## BLUEBERRY VINEGAR

This vinegar makes the simplest salad an epicurean delight. Try it on your Super Salads and taste the heightened flavor of all the vegetables.

1 cup red wine vinegar
¾ cup water
1 teaspoon sugar
1 cup fresh or unsweetened frozen blueberries,
    crushed lightly in a bowl
3 packages Equal (low-calorie sweetener)

Combine the vinegar, water, and sugar in a small saucepan. Stir until the sugar is completely dissolved. Bring the mixture to a boil and immediately pour it over the crushed fruit. Stir in the Equal. Cover the bowl with a clean dish towel and let it stand at least 2 hours.

Pour the vinegar into clean bottles or jars. Close tightly and store in the refrigerator for at least 1 week before using.

*Yield: approximately 3½ cups*
*Calories per tablespoon: 3*

## BOYSENBERRY VINEGAR

This dressing is particularly good when you sprinkle a little Equal (low-calorie sweetener) over the fruit or cottage cheese salads on which you use it. The acidity of the vinegar reacts most favorably with the sweetening element.

1 cup red wine vinegar
¾ cup water
1 teaspoon sugar
1 cup fresh or unsweetened frozen boysenberries, in
    a clean 1-quart screw-top jar

Combine the vinegar, water, and sugar in a small saucepan. Stir until the sugar is dissolved.

Bring the mixture to a boil and pour it over the berries. Cover the jar with a clean dish towel and let it stand for 2 hours.

Close the jar tightly and store it in the refrigerator for at least 48 hours before using.

*Yield: approximately 2½ cups*
*Calories per tablespoon: 3*

## ORANGE-SPICE VINEGAR

Sprinkle this vinegar over carrots and other steamed vegetables or bland fish. It makes a simple dish taste extra special.

Rind of 1 orange, cut in 1 long strip
2 cups white wine vinegar
¾ cup water
1 teaspoon sugar
3 packages Equal (low-calorie sweetener)
1 stick cinnamon

Remove all the white pulp from the orange rind and thread the rind onto a small wooden skewer if you have one.

Combine the vinegar, water, and sugar in a small saucepan. Bring the mixture just to a boil and immediately remove it from the heat. Stir in the Equal until it dissolves.

Place the rind and cinnamon stick in a clean jar for which you have a tight-fitting cover. Pour the hot mixture into the jar. Cool it to room temperature and cover. Steep for at least 48 hours before using.

*Yield: approximately 2½ cups*
*Calories per tablespoon: 1*

## MOCK MAYONNAISE

4 tablespoons diet mayonnaise
1 cup low-fat cottage cheese
½ tablespoon tarragon vinegar
½ tablespoon freshly squeezed lemon juice
½ tablespoon Dijon mustard
½ teaspoon Equal (low-calorie sweetener)

Combine all the ingredients in a blender jar and process at high speed 2 minutes or until the cottage cheese has been puréed. Process at low speed 1 minute longer. If the mixture is too thick, add skim milk, 1 tablespoon at a time, and process, but be careful not to make it too thin.

*Yield:  approximately 1½ cups*
*Calories per tablespoon: 16*

## ADRIANE'S DRESSING

This very low-calorie dressing is easy to prepare and will keep fresh in the refrigerator for at least a week. Try it to flavor any Super Salad or as a spread for lunch sandwiches.

> 1 cup plain low-fat yogurt
> 1 tablespoon Dijon mustard
> 1 tablespoon Orange Spice Vinegar (page 25)
> 2 packages Equal (low-calorie sweetener)
> Pinch salt

Combine all the ingredients in a small bowl and whisk until they are completely blended. Cover the bowl with plastic wrap and refrigerate.

Keep refrigerated when not in use.

> *Yield: 1 cup*
> *Calories per tablespoon: approximately 5*

## CUCUMBER-DILL DRESSING

You'll find yourself using this lovely dressing often on your salads, vegetables, and poached or baked fish or chicken. It has a clean, tart flavor that you're bound to enjoy.

The prepared dressing will keep for a week or slightly longer in the refrigerator.

> 1 medium cucumber, peeled and seeded
> ½ teaspoon salt
> 1 cup plain low-fat yogurt
> 2 tablespoons freshly squeezed lemon juice
> ½ teaspoon dried dill weed *or* 1 teaspoon fresh
> Pinch ground cumin
> ⅛ teaspoon freshly ground black pepper
> Equal (low-calorie sweetener) to taste (optional)

Slice the cucumber thinly and sprinkle with salt. Place in a strainer or colander and let drain 20 minutes. Squeeze out as much liquid as possible and chop fine. Set aside.

Combine the yogurt, juice, dill, cumin, and pepper in a small bowl. Whisk 1 minute. Add the cucumber and mix thoroughly. Sweeten if desired.

Keep covered in the refrigerator until needed. Stir before using.

*Yield: approximately 1¼ cups*
*Calories per tablespoon: 8*

## HOMEMADE SOUR HALF-AND-HALF

If you keep this dressing well refrigerated it will stay fresh for several weeks. Unlike the commercial variety it continues to sour slightly and begins to take on the flavor of real *crème fraîche.*

1 pint half-and-half
1 tablespoon plus 1 teaspoon buttermilk

Combine the half-and-half and buttermilk in a screw-top jar. Close the top tightly and shake the jar vigorously for 1 minute (not 1 second less). Set in a warm spot (an oven with a pilot light is ideal) for 24 hours. Refrigerate for at least 48 hours before serving, and always keep it refrigerated when it's not being used.

*Yield: approximately 2 cups*
*Calories per tablespoon: 20*

᭓ *When you absolutely must eat some-*
*thing sweet and have nothing at*
*home, try a tablespoon of jam or*
*jelly on crackers or toast. If all else*
*fails, drink tea with sugar or honey.*

## COTTAGE CHEESE SPRINKLE

Sprinkle a little of this blend of vegetables, herbs, and spices over your cottage cheese, salads, and cooked vegetables for a new and interesting taste treat.

2 tablespoons dried vegetable flakes
½ teaspoon chili powder
¼ teaspoon coarse salt
⅛ teaspoon ground cumin
⅛ teaspoon paprika
1 tablespoon sesame seeds, toasted

Combine the flakes, chili, salt, cumin, and paprika in a mortar and pestle. Grind to a fine powder. Add the sesame seeds and grind coarsely.

Keep in a screw-top jar, tightly covered, until needed.

*Yield: approximately 3 tablespoons*
*Calories per tablespoon: trace*

## BRAN-AND-SPICE SPRINKLE

Sprinkle a teaspoon of this tasty mix over your cottage cheese and yogurt and you add not only flavor but also the ever-necessary fiber. This mixture is sweet, so you might want to try it over fruits like strawberries and pineapple.

Because this sprinkle contains raw bran it's a good idea to keep it refrigerated when you are not using it.

Most supermarkets carry prepackaged raw bran, but if you have access to a health or natural food store, you can buy just the amount you need.

½ cup raw bran
½ teaspoon ground cinnamon
⅛ teaspoon ground mace
4 packages Equal (low-calorie sweetener)
Grated rind of 1 orange

Combine all the ingredients in a glass or metal bowl and toss to mix thoroughly.

Store in the refrigerator in a tightly closed screw-top jar until needed.

Shake well before using.

*Yield:  approximately 25 teaspoons*
*Calories per tablespoon: trace*

# PART II

---

# *The Recipes and Menu Plans*

# 5

## Pasta

### Easiest Pasta

This dinner is one to whip up after a hard day at the office, on the tennis court, shopping, or wherever. It takes practically no longer to prepare than the time it takes to cook the pasta. You'll love it!

> 2 cloves garlic, crushed or minced fine
> 1½ tablespoons olive oil
> 14 ounces Superoni spaghetti
> 3 medium eggs at room temperature, slightly beaten
>     with 1 teaspoon low-fat milk
> Salt and pepper to taste
> ¼ cup chopped parsley
> 2 ounces Parmesan cheese, grated

Combine the garlic and oil and set aside for 15 minutes.

Cook the spaghetti, being careful not to overcook. Drain thoroughly and return it to the pot.

Shaking the pan over low heat, "dry" the pasta. Add the oil and garlic and toss gently. Add the eggs and toss. The heat of the spaghetti should cook the eggs. Season to taste.

Transfer the pasta to a well-heated serving platter, sprinkle with the parsley and cheese, toss, and serve immediately.

*Yield: 6 diet servings*
*Calories per serving: 356*

## *EASIEST PASTA MENU PLAN*

*897 Calories (plus 200-calorie snack)*

Coffee, tea, or noncaloric beverages as desired

### BREAKFAST

1 slice frozen French toast
½ cup low-fat cottage cheese
½ cup fresh or unsweetened frozen strawberries

(*Substitute:* Basic Breakfast 4)

### LUNCH

Stuffed Pepper
1 large green pepper
2 ounces water-packed tuna
½ tomato, chopped
1 scallion, chopped (optional)
1 tablespoon diet mayonnaise
1 1-ounce whole wheat bread pocket
1 cup skim milk

(*Substitute:* Basic Lunch 3)

### DINNER

1 diet serving Easiest Pasta
1 serving Super Spinach Salad

## *Neapolitan Stuffed Peppers*

This Italian variation of the old standby can be prepared ahead and baked just before serving time. It can also be eaten at room temperature or as a cold entrée on a warm evening. If you wish to freeze the peppers, don't bake them. Place them on a baking sheet and freeze them. Wrap each one in freezer wrap and they will keep well.

Bake the frozen peppers 40 to 45 minutes.

> 8 large red bell peppers with flat broad bottoms
> 4 medium tomatoes, peeled and seeded
> 1 clove garlic, sliced
> 4 tablespoons chopped parsley
> 1 tablespoon tomato paste
> 4 black Italian or Greek olives, pitted (optional)
> 4 eggs, well beaten
> Salt and coarse freshly ground black pepper to taste
> 6 ounces orzo pasta, cooked and drained
> Nonstick vegetable oil spray

Slice off the top of each bell pepper and scoop out the seeds and membranes with a sharp spoon. Save the tops and do not break through the walls of the peppers.

Bring a large pot of water to a rolling boil and immerse the peppers and tops. Remove the pot from the stove and blanch the peppers and tops 1 minute. Remove them from the water with a slotted spoon and drain.

Quarter the tomatoes. Place them in a blender or food processor fitted with a metal blade. Add the garlic, parsley, tomato paste, and olives. Purée. Turn into a small bowl, add the eggs, and mix thoroughly. Add salt and pepper to taste.

Combine the pasta and sauce and toss. Fill each pepper with the pasta.

Spray a baking dish with nonstick vegetable oil; transfer the filled peppers to it and cover each with its top. Bake 25 minutes in a preheated 375°F oven.

*Yield: 4 diet servings*
*Calories per serving: 339*

## *NEAPOLITAN STUFFED PEPPERS MENU PLAN*

*900 Calories (plus 200-calorie snack)*

Coffee, tea, or noncaloric beverages as desired

### BREAKFAST

½ cup unsweetened pineapple chunks
½ cup low-fat cottage cheese
1 slice raisin bread toast

(*Substitute:* Basic Breakfast 1)

### LUNCH

Tomato-Tuna Pocket
    1 large tomato, chopped
    2 ounces water-packed tuna
    ½ green pepper, chopped
    1 scallion (optional)
    1 tablespoon diet mayonnaise
    1 1-ounce whole wheat bread pocket
1 cup skim milk

(*Substitute:* Basic Lunch 3)

### DINNER

1 diet serving Neapolitan Stuffed Peppers
½ serving Basic Super Salad
½ cup skim milk

## Zucchini Spaghetti

Measure out your diet portion and let your family or friends divide the rest. There won't be any leftovers.

3 medium zucchini, washed and trimmed
12 ounces Superoni spaghetti
3 tomatoes, peeled, seeded, and chopped coarsely
1 tablespoon whipped butter *or* diet margarine
1 medium onion, peeled, quartered, and thinly
  sliced
1 clove garlic, minced
2 tablespoons dry vermouth
3 fresh basil leaves, chopped, *or* ½ teaspoon dried
4 tablespoons chopped parsley
½ teaspoon salt
¼ teaspoon freshly ground black pepper
3 tablespoons grated Parmesan cheese

Shred the zucchini in a food processor or with a hand grater. Blanch it in boiling water for 30 seconds and drain thoroughly.

Cook the spaghetti.

Meanwhile, heat a large nonstick skillet. Add the tomatoes and cook, stirring, 1 minute. Add the butter, onions, and garlic and cook, stirring, 3 minutes. Add the zucchini, vermouth, basil, parsley, salt, and pepper. Stir and cook, covered, 3 to 5 minutes or until the vegetables are tender. Do not overcook. Their color should remain brilliant. If the skillet contains more than 2 tablespoons of liquid, increase the heat, uncover the pan, and cook, stirring, until the liquid is reduced.

Drain the pasta well and transfer it to a hot serving bowl. Top with the vegetables; toss, correct seasoning, and sprinkle with cheese.

Serve immediately.

*Yield: 6 diet servings*
*Calories per serving: 259*

## *ZUCCHINI SPAGHETTI MENU PLAN*

*914 Calories (plus 200-calorie snack)*

Coffee, tea, or noncaloric beverages as desired

### BREAKFAST

1 small banana
½ cup plain low-fat yogurt
1 slice whole wheat toast

(*Substitute:* Basic Breakfast 2)

### LUNCH

Salade Niçoise
    1 cup shredded romaine *or* loose-leafed
      lettuce
    1 hard-boiled egg
    2 ounces water-packed tuna
    1 ounce black olives
    ½ sweet red *or* green pepper
    1 or 2 slices red onion (optional)
    2 tablespoons chopped parsley
    1 tablespoon diet salad dressing
1 rice cake
½ cup skim milk

(*Substitute:* Basic Lunch 1)

### DINNER

1 diet serving Zucchini Spaghetti
½ serving Super Spinach Salad
1 cup skim milk

## Summer Macaroni Salad

A quick, easy, satisfying meal for any summer day. Serve the macaroni on or alongside a serving of Super Spinach Salad for a truly beautiful dinner.

½ cup Mock Mayonnaise (page 26)
¼ cup low-fat milk
1½ packages Equal (low-calorie sweetener)
4 tablespoons Blueberry Vinegar (page 24)
    or wine vinegar
8 ounces Superoni elbow macaroni, cooked and
    drained
5 hard-boiled medium eggs, coarsely chopped
6 inner stalks celery, chopped
1 small sweet red pepper, seeded and cut into thin
    strips
1 cup coarsely chopped zucchini
4 scallions, white and green parts, trimmed and
    finely chopped
10 stuffed Spanish olives, sliced
Salt and freshly ground black pepper to taste
6 large red radishes, sliced
Parsley sprigs for garnish

Whisk the "mayonnaise," milk, Equal, and vinegar together in a small mixing bowl. Reserve.

Combine the cooled macaroni, eggs, celery, pepper, zucchini, scallions, and olives in a large mixing bowl. Toss gently.

Pour the dressing over the salad. Toss, correct seasoning, and chill.

Garnish with radishes and parsley.

*Yield: 6 diet servings*
*Calories per serving: 254*

## *SUMMER MACARONI SALAD MENU PLAN*
### *900 Calories (plus 200-calorie snack)*

Coffee, tea, or noncaloric beverages as desired

## BREAKFAST

1 frozen cheese blintz, cooked in a nonstick
   skillet and served with
½ cup artificially sweetened low-fat yogurt
1 cup fresh or unsweetened frozen strawberries
   *or* ½ cup sliced bananas

(*Substitute:* Basic Breakfast 1)

## LUNCH

Tostada with Chicken
   2 frozen corn tortillas, heated in nonstick
      pan
   2½ ounces chicken, shredded
   ½ cup shredded romaine lettuce
   ½ cup chopped tomatoes
   ½ green pepper, chopped
   Salsa to taste
1 cup skim milk

(*Substitute:* Basic Lunch 2)

## DINNER

1 diet serving Summer Macaroni Salad
1 serving Super Spinach Salad
1 cup cooked carrots, sprinkled with dill

## Pasta e Fagioli

Be sure to refrigerate leftover portions. They're delicious served cold.

> Nonstick vegetable oil spray
> 1 tablespoon whipped butter *or* diet margarine
> 1 clove garlic, peeled and minced
> 1 small shallot, peeled and minced
> 1 inner stalk celery with leaves, thinly sliced
> 1 medium carrot, scraped and finely minced
> 4 tomatoes, peeled, seeded, and coarsely chopped
> 1 16-ounce can kidney beans
> 6 ounces Superoni small macaroni, cooked until tender but not soft, and drained
> 1 6-ounce can vegetable cocktail juice
> ¼ teaspoon dried oregano *or* ½ teaspoon fresh
> 4 tablespoons chopped parsley

Spray a nonstick skillet lightly with nonstick vegetable oil. Add the butter and melt over low heat. Combine the garlic and shallots and add to the skillet. Sauté, stirring, until soft. Add the celery, carrots, and tomatoes. Cook, stirring occasionally, 3 minutes.

Meanwhile, combine the beans and their liquid, pasta, juice, oregano in a 3-quart saucepan and add the sautéed vegetables when they are done.

Bring to a boil, reduce the heat, cover, and simmer 5 minutes. Taste, correct seasoning, and cook, uncovered, over medium-high heat, until the liquid is reduced by half.

Sprinkle with parsley.

*Yield: 4 diet servings*
*Calories per serving: 357*

## *PASTA E FAGIOLI MEAL PLAN*

*920 Calories (plus 200-calorie snack)*

Coffee, tea, or noncaloric beverages as desired

### BREAKFAST

1 cup cooked oatmeal
1 tablespoon raisins
½ cup skim milk

(*Substitute:* Basic Breakfast 3)

### LUNCH

Fruit Salad
    1 cup shredded romaine lettuce
    1 cup low-fat cottage cheese
    1 cup cut-up cantaloupe *or* 1 small banana
1 slice whole wheat bread

(*Substitute:* Basic Lunch 2)

### DINNER

1 diet serving Pasta e Fagioli
½ cup skim milk

᳝ *Don't brood about having to give up foods that are too fattening for the diet. Think of them as belonging to a phase in your life that you have outgrown. After all, do you still eat baby food?*

## *Venetian Pasta and Beans*

The use of oriental spices in Venetian cooking is not as strange as it seems. Venice was one of the great trading nations in the Middle Ages and spices like cinnamon, cardamon, and cumin made their way into Venetian cooking at that time.

> Nonstick vegetable oil spray
> 1 tablespoon olive oil
> 1 large onion, chopped coarsely
> 1 16-ounce can kidney beans
> ⅛ teaspoon cinnamon
> ½ teaspoon coarse salt
> ½ teaspoon freshly ground pepper
> 4 beef bouillon cubes, dissolved in 4 cups boiling
>   water
> 1 cup small pasta shells
> 1 tablespoon soybean "bacon bits"
> 2 tablespoons grated Parmesan cheese

Spray a 2-quart nonstick saucepan with nonstick vegetable oil. Add the olive oil and onion and cook gently over moderate heat, stirring, until golden.

Add the beans and their liquid, cinnamon, salt, pepper, and bouillon and bring to a boil.

Cover, reduce heat to moderate-low, and simmer 40 minutes. Add shells and cook an additional 12 to 16 minutes.

Stir in "bacon bits." Sprinkle with cheese.

> *Yield: 4 diet servings*
> *Calories per serving: 203*

## *VENETIAN PASTA AND BEANS MENU PLAN*

*903 Calories (plus 200-calorie snack)*

Coffee, tea, or noncaloric beverages as desired

## BREAKFAST

½ grapefruit
1 poached egg
½ whole wheat English muffin

(*Substitute:* Basic Breakfast 2)

## LUNCH

Tostada with Chicken
2 frozen corn tortillas, heated in nonstick
pan
2½ ounces chicken, shredded
½ cup shredded romaine lettuce
½ cup chopped tomatoes
½ green pepper, chopped
Salsa to taste
1 cup skim milk

(*Substitute:* Basic Lunch 1)

## DINNER

1 diet serving Venetian Pasta and Beans
½ serving Super Spinach Salad
1 cup skim milk

## *Cold Pasta e Fagioli*

In most areas of Italy this dish is served as a thick soup. This southern Italian version makes a delicious meal-in-a-dish that's perfect for hot summer evenings.

    2 tablespoons olive oil
    2 cloves garlic, bruised
    2 tablespoons minced sweet red pepper
    4 anchovy fillets, mashed
    1 teaspoon chopped capers
    10 ripe pitted black olives, sliced
    3 very ripe tomatoes, peeled, seeded, and chopped
    1 teaspoon freshly squeezed lemon juice
    1 medium bay leaf
    ⅛ teaspoon dried oregano
    1 cup canned white kidney beans, drained
    Salt and pepper to taste
    6 ounces Superoni macaroni
    2 tablespoons chopped parsley

Heat the oil in a saucepan. Add the garlic and peppers. Sauté 1 minute.

Combine the anchovies, capers, and olives in a small bowl. Stir into the saucepan and sauté, stirring, until the garlic is golden. Discard the garlic. Add the tomatoes, lemon juice, bay leaf, and oregano. Bring to a boil, reduce the heat, and simmer about 10 minutes. Add the beans, correct seasoning with salt and pepper, and stir. Continue to simmer 5 minutes longer.

Meanwhile, cook the pasta, drain, and turn into a serving bowl. (Be certain that the pasta is very dry.) Pour the beans and sauce over the pasta, discard the bay leaf, and toss gently.

Sprinkle with parsley and chill.

*Yield: 6 diet servings*
*Calories per serving: 290*

## COLD PASTA E FAGIOLI MENU PLAN
*886 Calories (plus 200-calorie snack)*

Coffee, tea, or noncaloric beverages as desired

### BREAKFAST

1 frozen waffle, spread with
¼ cup low-fat cottage cheese, sprinkled with
1 tablespoon wheat germ, mixed with
1 teaspoon cinnamon sugar
½ banana

(*Substitute:* Basic Breakfast 1)

### LUNCH

Tostada with Cheese
    2 frozen corn tortillas, heated in nonstick
      pan
    2 ounces Lite-line cheese, shredded
    ½ green pepper, chopped
    ½ medium tomato, chopped
    Salsa to taste
1 cup skim milk

(*Substitute:* Basic Lunch 3)

### DINNER

1 diet serving Cold Pasta e Fagioli
½ serving any Super Salad
½ cup skim milk

## *Spaghetti con Ceci*

If you are one of the millions of people who love cold pasta salads, serve any leftovers cold with a teaspoon of tarragon vinegar and you will have two treats for the work of one.

> 2 large, very ripe tomatoes (1 pound total)
> 1 tablespoon tomato paste
> ½ teaspoon coarse salt
> 2 black peppercorns, crushed well
> ½ cup fresh basil (may be omitted if not available)
> ½ cup fresh parsley
> 1 small clove garlic, minced
> 1 tablespoon olive oil
> 8 ounces Superoni spaghetti, cooked and drained
>     thoroughly
> 1 cup canned chickpeas, heated in their own liquid
>     and drained
> 2 ounces imported Parmesan cheese, grated

Chop the tomatoes coarsely. Combine the tomatoes with the tomato paste, salt, pepper, basil, parsley, and garlic in a blender or food processor fitted with a metal blade. Purée. Add the oil and turn the blender on and off twice.

Place the thoroughly drained pasta in a serving bowl, add the thoroughly drained chickpeas, and toss.

Add half of the sauce, toss, and taste. Pour the remaining sauce over the pasta and sprinkle with the cheese.

> *Yield: 6 diet servings*
> *Calories per serving: 249*

### *SPAGHETTI CON CECI MENU PLAN*
*883 Calories (plus 200-calorie snack)*

Coffee, tea, or noncaloric beverages as desired

**BREAKFAST**

1 slice frozen French toast
1 poached egg
½ cup skim milk

(*Substitute:* Basic Breakfast 4)

**LUNCH**

Wry Cheese
2 ounces Lite-line cheese
2 slices rye toast
Mustard *or* 1 tablespoon diet margarine *or*
diet mayonnaise
½ cup skim milk

(*Substitute:* Basic Lunch 2)

**DINNER**

1 diet serving Spaghetti con Ceci
1 serving any Super Salad
1 cup fresh or unsweetened frozen strawberries

❧ *As you shrink, so will your food budget. Use the leftover money to reward yourself with something pleasurable for staying on the diet.*

## *Pasta with Lima Beans*

A quick and easy to prepare dish that repays your effort ten-fold in taste.

> 8 ounces Superoni ziti *or* elbow macaroni
> Nonstick vegetable oil spray
> 1 package frozen baby lima beans
> 1 tablespoon olive oil
> 1 medium onion, halved lengthwise and thinly
>   sliced
> 1 clove garlic, finely minced
> ½ teaspoon dried savory
> 4 tablespoons finely chopped parsley
> ½ teaspoon coarse salt
> ⅛ teaspoon freshly ground black pepper
> 2 tablespoons hot water

Cook the pasta and drain.

Spray a nonstick skillet with nonstick vegetable oil. Set aside.

Cook the lima beans until they are tender but still quite firm. Drain and set aside.

Heat the oil in the skillet. Add the onion and garlic and sauté, stirring until soft. Add the lima beans, savory, 3 tablespoons parsley, salt, pepper, and 2 tablespoons hot water. Cook, covered, 3 to 5 minutes or until the beans are soft but not mushy.

Combine the pasta and beans, toss, and garnish with the remaining chopped parsley.

Serve immediately or cool, chill, and serve cold.

*Yield: 6 diet servings*
*Calories per serving: 277*

# PASTA WITH LIMA BEANS MENU PLAN

*899 Calories (plus 200-calorie snack)*

Coffee, tea, or noncaloric beverages as desired

## BREAKFAST

1 frozen waffle, topped with
½ cup low-fat cottage cheese and
½ banana, sliced

(*Substitute:* Basic Breakfast 4)

## LUNCH

Turkey Pocket
2 ounces turkey
½ cucumber, chopped
1 scallion, chopped
1 tablespoon diet mayonnaise
Fresh or dried dill to taste
1 1-ounce whole wheat bread pocket

(*Substitute:* Basic Lunch 3)

## DINNER

1 diet serving Pasta with Lima Beans
1 serving any Super Salad
½ cup skim milk

## *Piquant Chicken Casserole*

To get the maximum flavor from this dish it's best to eat it soon after preparation. It may be baked and reheated in the oven, but be prepared to sacrifice some moisture.

Nonstick vegetable oil spray
1 tablespoon olive oil
½ pound fresh mushrooms, thinly sliced
1 medium onion, chopped
½ green pepper, finely chopped
4 tablespoons instant flour
1½ cups low-fat milk
½ cup dry white wine
½ cup dry sherry
1 tablespoon Worcestershire sauce
1 teaspoon salt
¼ teaspoon freshly ground black pepper
1 package frozen cooked diced chicken, thawed
4 ounces Superoni vermicelli *or* thin spaghetti, cooked
2 ounces mild cheddar cheese, grated
Chopped parsley for garnish (optional)

Prepare an attractive casserole by spraying the bottom and sides with nonstick vegetable oil. Set aside.

Heat the oil in a nonstick saucepan. Add the mushrooms, onions, and green pepper. Sauté, stirring, until the vegetables are soft and their juices extracted.

Sprinkle in the flour and blend thoroughly. Add the milk, wines, Worcestershire sauce, salt, and pepper and cook over very low heat until the sauce thickens — about 10 minutes. Stir occasionally to prevent lumps.

Add the chicken, pasta, and half the cheese to the thickened sauce. Mix thoroughly.

Turn the mixture into the prepared casserole and sprinkle

with the remaining cheese. Cover and bake 30 minutes in a
preheated 375°F oven.

Garnish with parsley and serve from the casserole.

*Yield: 6 diet servings*
*Calories per serving: 302*

---

### PIQUANT CHICKEN CASSEROLE
### MENU PLAN

*892 Calories (plus 200-calorie snack)*

Coffee, tea, or noncaloric beverages as desired

### BREAKFAST

1 small orange, sliced
⅔ cup cooked Wheatena
1 teaspoon cinnamon sugar
½ cup skim milk

(*Substitute:* Basic Breakfast 3)

### LUNCH

1 cup shredded romaine lettuce or escarole
½ cup low-fat cottage cheese
½ cup plain low-fat yogurt
1 cup fresh or unsweetened frozen strawberries
3 rice cakes

### DINNER

1 diet serving Piquant Chicken Casserole
½ serving any Super Salad
½ cup skim milk

## Velvety Casserole

This lovely casserole *must* be prepared ahead — at the very least, the night before. Keep it in the refrigerator, well covered, for no more than 3 or 4 days.

> 3 tablespoons whipped butter *or* diet margarine
> ½ pound mushrooms, scrubbed, trimmed, and sliced
> ½ onion, finely chopped
> 1 teaspoon coarse salt
> ¼ teaspoon freshly ground black pepper
> 2 packages frozen artichokes, cooked
> 2 cups frozen (thawed) cooked or leftover skinless chicken, diced
> 4 ounces Superoni elbow macaroni, cooked
> 1 cup canned condensed chicken broth, combined with 1 teaspoon freshly squeezed lemon juice
> 2 tablespoons cornstarch, softened in ¼ cup dry white wine
> ⅛ teaspoon dried marjoram
> 2 ounces imported Swiss cheese, grated
> 2 tablespoons dry sherry
> 2 ounces fresh French or Italian bread, grated into soft bread crumbs

Melt 2 tablespoons butter in a large nonstick skillet. Sauté mushrooms and onions until soft. Add salt and pepper; stir.

Combine the sautéed vegetables, artichokes, chicken, and macaroni in a 1½ or 2 quart casserole pretty enough to bring to the table. Mix well and set aside.

Combine the broth and softened cornstarch in a small saucepan and cook, stirring, until it is the consistency of heavy cream. Add the marjoram and cheese and continue stirring until the cheese melts. Stir in the sherry and pour this sauce over the chicken in the casserole.

Melt the remaining butter in a small saucepan, add the bread crumbs, and stir until the butter has been absorbed. Sprinkle the bread crumbs over the chicken and place the casserole in a preheated 375°F oven. Bake, uncovered, about 40 minutes. Remove, cool to room temperature, and cover. Refrigerate overnight. Reheat in a preheated 375°F oven.

*Yield: 6 diet servings*
*Calories per serving: 302*

---

### VELVETY CASSEROLE MENU PLAN

*905 Calories (plus 200-calorie snack)*

Coffee, tea, or noncaloric beverages as desired

**BREAKFAST** (*Substitute:* Basic Breakfast 1)
1 small orange
4 rice cakes
1 tablespoon diet jelly
1 cup skim milk

**LUNCH** (*Substitute:* Basic Lunch 1)
Tostada Melt
2 frozen corn tortillas, heated in nonstick pan
2 ounces water-packed tuna
1 ounce skim-milk mozzarella cheese
Melt under broiler.
1 carrot
½ green pepper
½ cup skim milk

**DINNER**
1 diet serving Velvety Casserole
½ serving any Super Salad
1 small tangerine
½ cup skim milk

## Chicken à l'Orange

Try this on dinner guests and then tell them it's on your diet. No one will believe anything that tastes so good can be so good for you.

> 3 whole chicken breasts, boned, skinned, all visible fat removed, and cut in half (1 pound 5 ounces)
> 3 tablespoons tarragon vinegar
> 1 tablespoon freshly squeezed lemon juice
> ½ teaspoon salt
> ⅛ teaspoon oregano
> ⅛ teaspoon rosemary
> ¼ teaspoon Equal (low-calorie sweetener)
> 1 tablespoon olive oil
> ½ small can unsweetened frozen orange juice, thawed but undiluted
> 8 ounces egg noodles

Place the chicken breasts in a small baking dish for which you have a cover.

Combine the vinegar, lemon juice, salt, oregano, rosemary, and Equal in a small mixing bowl. Whisk until the salt and Equal have dissolved. Add the oil and whisk until completely blended. Add the orange juice and mix thoroughly.

Pour the sauce over the chicken, cover, and bake 45 minutes in a preheated 350°F oven, basting occasionally.

Remove the cover, baste, and bake an additional 15 minutes, basting frequently, to brown.

Cook the noodles. Place one half breast on a bed of noodles and spoon some sauce over it. May be garnished with a thin slice of orange sprinkled with chopped parsley.

*Yield: 6 diet servings*
*Calories per serving: 298*

## CHICKEN À L'ORANGE MENU PLAN

*900 Calories (plus 200-calorie snack)*

Coffee, tea, or noncaloric beverages as desired

### BREAKFAST

½ cup fresh or unsweetened frozen strawberries
1 slice cooked lean ham
1 slice frozen French toast
½ cup skim milk

(*Substitute:* Basic Breakfast 2)

### LUNCH

Green and White Tomato
   1 large tomato, stuffed with
      5 ounces tofu
      1 tablespoon chopped parsley
      1 scallion, chopped
      1 tablespoon diet salad dressing
1 1-ounce whole wheat bread pocket, toasted

(*Substitute:* Basic Lunch 2)

### DINNER

1 diet serving Chicken à l'Orange
1 cup cooked broccoli
½ serving Basic Super Salad
½ cup skim milk

## *Chicken Pasta Mandorla*

The subtle hint of almonds transforms this simple chicken noodle casserole into a party dish.

Because this recipe calls for frozen chicken it is not a good idea to refreeze it. However, you may refrigerate the leftovers and serve them hot or cold the following day or two.

> Nonstick vegetable oil spray
> 8 ounces Superoni fettuccine, cooked
> 1 ounce almonds, slivered
> ¾ cup evaporated low-fat milk
> 1 can condensed cream of chicken soup
> ¼ teaspoon salt
> ¼ teaspoon almond extract
> 2 ounces sharp cheddar cheese, finely shredded
> 1 cup celery, diced
> ½ cup sweet red pepper, blanched and diced
> 2 cups frozen (thawed) cooked or leftover skinless
>     chicken, diced
> 3 tablespoons seasoned bread crumbs
> 1 tablespoon whipped butter *or* diet margarine

Prepare a shallow casserole or baking dish by spraying the bottom and sides with nonstick vegetable oil. Arrange the cooked fettuccine on the bottom and set aside.

Brown the almonds slightly in a small, heavy-bottomed, dry skillet, shaking the pan continually. Do not let them burn. Remove from the pan and reserve.

Combine the milk and soup in a saucepan and stir to mix thoroughly. Add the salt and extract. Stirring constantly, heat just to the boiling point. Remove from the heat, add the cheese, and stir until melted. Add the celery, red pepper, and chicken. Return to the heat and cook, stirring, 1 minute longer.

Pour the chicken mixture over the fettuccine; sprinkle with the bread crumbs and almonds and moisten the top with melted butter.

Place in a preheated 400°F oven, uncovered, and bake 20 to 25 minutes until brown and heated through.

*Yield: 6 diet servings*
*Calories per serving: 257*

---

### CHICKEN PASTA MANDORLA MENU PLAN

*905 Calories (plus 200-calorie snack)*

Coffee, tea, or noncaloric beverages as desired

### BREAKFAST

1 cup vanilla-flavored low-fat yogurt
1 teaspoon wheat germ

(*Substitute:* Basic Breakfast 1)

### LUNCH

Chop-Chop Egg
    1 hard-boiled egg, chopped
    ½ cucumber, chopped
    1 scallion, chopped (optional)
    1 small tomato, chopped
    1 teaspoon diet mayonnaise
1 1-ounce whole wheat bread pocket
1 cup skim milk

### DINNER

1 diet serving Chicken Pasta Mandorla
1 serving Super Spinach Salad
1 cup fresh or unsweetened frozen strawberries
2 small plain bread sticks

## *Divine Chicken*

This casserole may be prepared ahead of time and refrigerated.

> Nonstick vegetable oil spray
> 8 ounces chicken breast, boned and skinned
> 1 chicken bouillon cube in ½ cup boiling water
> ½ teaspoon freshly squeezed lemon juice
> 8 ounces Superoni spaghetti, cooked and drained
> 3 tablespoons whipped butter *or* diet margarine
> 2 tablespoons all-purpose flour
> 1 cup low-fat milk, scalded
> ½ teaspoon salt
> ⅛ teaspoon white pepper
> Pinch nutmeg
> ½ pound mushrooms, scrubbed, trimmed, and sliced
> 1 cup frozen asparagus, cooked and cut into pieces
> 1 medium egg yolk, slightly beaten
> 1 ounce imported Parmesan cheese, grated
> 4 tablespoons seasoned bread crumbs

Prepare a medium casserole by spraying the bottom and sides with nonstick vegetable oil. Set aside.

Combine the chicken, all but 1 tablespoon of the bouillon, and the lemon juice in a small nonstick skillet. Bring to a boil, lower heat, cover, and poach until the chicken is cooked through. Remove the chicken and reserve the poaching liquid. Slice the chicken into thin strips. Cut up the spaghetti, mix with chicken and set aside.

Melt 2 tablespoons butter in a small nonstick saucepan. Stir in the flour. Stirring continuously, slowly add hot milk. Mix thoroughly. Add the salt, pepper, and nutmeg and cook, stirring, until the sauce is quite thick. Set aside.

Melt the remaining butter in a small nonstick skillet and stir in the remaining bouillon. Add the mushrooms and sauté over high heat. Combine with the asparagus.

Combine the chicken, pasta, vegetables, and sauce in a 3-quart nonstick or stainless-steel saucepan. Heat quickly, stirring gently. If the mixture appears too dry, add a tablespoon of reserved poaching liquid. Do not make it too moist. Remove from the heat, stir in the egg, and turn into the prepared casserole. Combine the cheese and bread crumbs and sprinkle over the top. Bake, covered, in a preheated 400°F oven for 20 to 30 minutes until brown and bubbling.

*Yield: 4 diet servings*
*Calories per serving: 381*

---

### DIVINE CHICKEN MENU PLAN

*927 Calories (plus 200-calorie snack)*
Coffee, tea, or noncaloric beverages as desired

**BREAKFAST**   (*Substitute:* Basic Breakfast 1)

    1 cup fortified cereal
    1 cup skim milk

**LUNCH**   (*Substitute:* Basic Lunch 3)

Ham and Cheese Pocket
    1 slice lean canned ham
    1 ounce Lite-line cheese
    1 green pepper, chopped
    1 tomato, sliced
    1 1-ounce whole wheat bread pocket
1 cup skim milk

**DINNER**

    1 diet serving Divine Chicken
    1 cup fresh or unsweetened frozen strawberries
    *or* 1 orange

## Pasticcio Chicken Livers

Chicken livers are a good source of iron, and this is a delightful way to prepare them.

Those who have elevated levels of cholesterol may want to avoid organ meats altogether. There are many other recipes to try instead.

> Nonstick vegetable oil spray
> 1 tablespoon olive oil
> 1 onion, finely chopped
> 1 inner stalk celery, finely chopped
> 1 leek, white part only, washed and finely chopped
> 1 small carrot, finely chopped
> 2 large tomatoes, peeled, seeded, and finely chopped
> Salt and pepper to taste
> ½ pound chicken livers, membranes removed, cut into small pieces
> 1 tablespoon whipped butter *or* diet margarine
> 8 ounces Superoni macaroni, cooked
> 3 ounces imported Parmesan cheese, grated

Prepare a baking dish or ovenproof casserole by spraying the bottom and sides with nonstick vegetable oil. Set aside.

Heat the olive oil in a nonstick skillet. Add the onion and brown slightly. Add the celery, leek, and carrot and cook until soft. Stir in the tomatoes and season with salt and pepper. Add the chicken livers and cook, stirring occasionally, 3 minutes.

Add the butter to the warm pasta and toss to cover. Add 2 tablespoons of the cheese and toss.

Put one layer of pasta on the bottom of the prepared baking dish, cover it with a layer of the chicken liver mixture, and sprinkle some cheese over it. Repeat this process until all the ingredients have been used, ending with a layer of pasta and a sprinkling of cheese.

Bake in a preheated 375°F oven about 10 minutes or until brown.

*Yield: 6 diet servings*
*Calories per serving: 310*

---

### PASTICCIO CHICKEN LIVER MENU PLAN
*904 Calories (plus 200-calorie snack)*

Coffee, tea, or noncaloric beverages as desired

**BREAKFAST**

½ cup fresh or unsweetened frozen strawberries

½ cup low-fat cottage cheese, mixed with
¼ cup plain low-fat yogurt
½ English muffin

(*Substitute:* Basic Breakfast 4)

**LUNCH**

Swiss Pocket
1 ounce Swiss cheese
1 tomato, chopped
1 1-ounce whole wheat bread pocket
1 cup skim milk

(*Substitute:* Basic Lunch 3)

**DINNER**

1 diet serving Pasticcio Chicken Livers
1 serving any Super Salad

## *Turkey-Noodle Capri*

Freeze this luscious casserole before baking, if you like. Bake the frozen dish, uncovered, in a preheated 350°F oven for 30 to 40 minutes or until heated through and bubbling.

> Nonstick vegetable oil spray
> 1 package frozen broccoli
> ½ cup broccoli cooking liquid
> 8 ounces broad noodles
> 1 can condensed cheddar cheese soup
> ½ teaspoon coarse salt
> ⅛ teaspoon freshly ground black pepper
> ⅛ teaspoon dry mustard
> 1 ounce cheddar cheese, grated
> 2 cups diced cooked turkey
> ½ ounce almonds, slivered

Prepare a large, attractive casserole by spraying the bottom and sides lightly with nonstick vegetable oil. Set aside.

Cook the broccoli, drain, and reserve vegetable and liquid separately. Then cook the noodles, drain, and set aside.

Mix the soup, broccoli liquid, salt, pepper, and mustard in a small saucepan; stir and heat. Add the cheese and cook, stirring, until the cheese melts and the sauce is thick.

Combine the noodles and sauce in a large bowl, and arrange half in the prepared casserole. Arrange a layer of turkey over the noodles, then a layer of broccoli; repeat until all is used. Cover with the remaining noodles and sprinkle with almonds.

Bake, uncovered, in a preheated 350°F oven for 20 minutes or until the food bubbles.

Serve from the casserole.

> *Yield: 6 diet servings*
> *Calories per serving: 307*

## TURKEY-NOODLE CAPRI MENU PLAN

*895 Calories (plus 200-calorie snack)*

Coffee, tea, or noncaloric beverages as desired

### BREAKFAST

½ cup orange juice
½ cup cooked hot cereal
1 cup skim milk

(*Substitute:* Basic Breakfast 1)

### LUNCH

Cucumber Boats
    1 large cucumber, seeded and filled with
    1 cup low-fat cottage cheese, mixed with
    1 tablespoon dry onion soup mix
    1 scallion, chopped
    ½ cup chopped green pepper
    1 tablespoon chopped parsley
1 English muffin, toasted

(*Substitute:* Basic Lunch 4)

### DINNER

1 diet serving Turkey-Noodle Capri
½ serving Basic Super Salad
1 small tangerine

*Do you sit around the house on Saturdays, nibbling? Go to the library, where eating is forbidden.*

## *Stir-Fry Turkey Crunch*

Although this dish tastes best right after it has been cooked, it is also good as leftovers and can be frozen in individual serving containers. To reheat portions after freezing, add a little water to the bottom of the saucepan. Do not overcook.

1½ cups fresh or canned bean sprouts, drained
1 tablespoon whipped butter *or* diet margarine
1 medium onion, thinly sliced
1 package frozen green peas, cooked just until barely tender
1 sweet red pepper, seeded, blanched, and coarsely chopped
1 cup celery, sliced
8 canned water chestnuts, sliced
1½ cups diced cooked turkey
4 ounces thin noodles, cooked and cut into small pieces
½ cup canned condensed chicken broth
¼ teaspoon salt
¼ teaspoon sugar
¼ teaspoon grated ginger
2 tablespoons cornstarch, softened in 4 tablespoons bourbon *or* scotch whiskey (water may be substituted)
2 tablespoons soy sauce

Soak the bean sprouts in ice water to crisp.

Melt the butter in a large nonstick skillet and sauté the onions until soft, not brown. Add the peas, pepper, celery, water chestnuts, turkey, noodles, and broth. Bring the broth to a boil.

Combine the salt, sugar, ginger, cornstarch/whiskey, and soy sauce. Mix thoroughly until the salt and sugar have dissolved. Add to the skillet, stirring, and cook until the sauce thickens.

Drain the bean sprouts thoroughly, add to the skillet, and stir in gently. Cook 1 minute to heat.

*Yield: 6 diet servings*
*Calories per serving: 267*

---

### STIR-FRY TURKEY CRUNCH MENU PLAN

*907 Calories (plus 200-calorie snack)*
Coffee, tea, or noncaloric beverages as desired

#### BREAKFAST

½ cup grapefruit juice
1 frozen waffle, sprinkled with
1 tablespoon wheat germ, mixed with
1 teaspoon cinnamon sugar

(*Substitute:* Basic Breakfast 1)

#### LUNCH

Romaine Rolls
    4 large romaine lettuce leaves, rolled around
    3 ounces water-packed tuna, mixed with
    1 scallion, chopped
    ½ cucumber, chopped
    1 tablespoon diet mayonnaise
3 rice cakes
1 cup skim milk

(*Substitute:* Basic Lunch 3)

#### DINNER

1 diet serving Stir-Fry Turkey Crunch
1 serving any Super Salad
½ cup skim milk

# Turkey Ragout

This ragout may be frozen in individual containers and re-heated when desired. If you freeze it, be sure to undercook the fettuccine slightly, so you have firm, not mushy, pasta when you defrost it.

> 1 tablespoon olive oil
> 1 pound turkey cutlets, cut into ½-inch strips
> 3 large onions, thinly sliced
> 4 cloves garlic, put through garlic press
> 1 teaspoon curry powder
> 2 cups water
> 1 cup dry white wine
> 1 can condensed cream of tomato soup
> Salt to taste
> ¾ pound mushrooms, sliced
> 6 ounces Superoni fettuccine, cooked just tender (*al dente*) and cut into small pieces

Heat the oil in a 3-quart saucepan over high heat. Add the turkey and onions, reduce the heat, and cook, stirring, until the onions are brown. Add the garlic and stir. Blend in the curry, water, wine, soup, and salt. Cover and simmer 40 minutes over very low heat.

Uncover, gently fold in the mushrooms and pasta, and simmer an additional 10 minutes. If the sauce is too thick for your taste, add 2 tablespoons of wine during the last 10 minutes of cooking. If too thin, increase the heat and cook, stirring, to reduce the sauce.

*Yield: 6 diet servings*
*Calories per serving: 324*

## TURKEY RAGOUT MENU PLAN
*902 Calories (plus 200-calorie snack)*

Coffee, tea, or noncaloric beverages as desired

### BREAKFAST

½ grapefruit
½ toasted bagel
1 slice skim-milk mozzarella cheese

(*Substitute:* Basic Breakfast 3)

### LUNCH

Tofu Crunch
    5 ounces tofu, combined with
    1 teaspoon soy sauce
    1 can chop suey vegetables *or* bean sprouts
    ½ green pepper, chopped
        Stir-fry in nonstick pan.
½ cup cooked rice *or* 2 rice cakes

(*Substitute:* Basic Lunch 2)

### DINNER

1 diet serving Turkey Ragout
1 cup cooked broccoli
1 serving any Super Salad
1 cup skim milk

❧ *It's amazing how much time you
can save in food preparation if your
knives are sharp.*

## *Braised Beef Burgundy*

This is a good recipe for a family of four with only one person on the diet. The nondieters' portions will be abundant and the whole family will thank you for a memorable meal.

> Nonstick vegetable oil spray
> 1 pound very lean round steak, all visible fat
> 　　trimmed, cut into 1½-inch cubes
> 4 carrots, thickly sliced
> 4 small boiling onions, quartered
> ½ pound mushrooms, sliced
> 4 inner stalks celery, chopped
> 1 medium can whole tomatoes
> 1 can condensed beef consommé
> ½ cup Burgundy wine
> Salt and freshly ground black pepper to taste
> 6 ounces noodles, cooked and drained
> Chopped parsley for garnish

Spray a nonstick skillet very lightly with nonstick vegetable oil and heat. Add the beef cubes and sear very quickly on all sides.

Turn the meat into a medium casserole. Add the carrots, onions, mushrooms, celery, tomatoes, consommé, and wine. Mix and season with salt and pepper.

Bake, covered, in a preheated 350°F oven for 1½ hours or until the meat is quite tender.

Arrange the noodles around the edges of a serving platter. Remove the meat and vegetables from the casserole with a slotted spoon, and place them in the center of the platter. If the sauce is too thin, turn it into a small saucepan and bring it to a boil. Reduce it slightly and spoon it over the meat. Garnish with parsley and serve. Pass the remaining sauce separately.

*Yield: 6 diet servings*
*Calories per serving: 284*

---

### *BRAISED BEEF BURGUNDY MENU PLAN*
*904 Calories (plus 200-calorie snack)*

Coffee, tea, or noncaloric beverages as desired

## BREAKFAST

½ banana, sliced, mixed with
½ cup low-fat cottage cheese, mixed with
¼ cup plain low-fat yogurt
2 Melba toast rounds

(*Substitute:* Basic Breakfast 4)

## LUNCH

Asparagus-Cheese Melt
1 English muffin, topped with
4 spears fresh or frozen asparagus
2 ounces Lite-line cheese
Melt under broiler.
1 carrot

(*Substitute:* Basic Lunch 3)

## DINNER

1 diet serving Braised Beef Burgundy
1 cup cooked broccoli
½ serving any Super Salad
½ cup skim milk

## *Indonesian Beef with Onions*

If you like Chinese food, you'll love this delicious dish. It's very easy to prepare, and because it contains so little hydrogenated fat, leftovers will keep well in the refrigerator for several days.

To prepare leftovers, reheat slowly and serve.

> 2 tablespoons sunflower *or* safflower oil
> 6 medium onions, peeled, halved, and very thinly sliced
> 1 clove garlic, minced
> ½ pound very lean ground beef
> 1 tablespoon soy sauce
> 1 teaspoon sugar
> 1 beef bouillon cube, dissolved in ¾ cup boiling water
> 2 teaspoons peanut butter
> 2 teaspoons sherry
> 7 ounces tofu, cut into 1-inch cubes
> 2 ounces Superoni vermicelli, cooked and cut into small pieces
> 2 teaspoons cornstarch

Heat 1 tablespoon of the oil in a seasoned wok or large nonstick skillet. Add the onions and garlic and sauté, stirring constantly, about 2 minutes or until transparent. Remove and set aside. Mix soy sauce, sugar, and beef. Set aside.

Heat the remaining oil in the wok and add the beef. Cook about 10 minutes, stirring occasionally. Add half the bouillon, the peanut butter, and the sherry, and stir. Gently fold in the tofu, vermicelli, and onions. Reduce the heat, cover, and cook an additional 5 minutes.

Combine the remaining broth with the cornstarch and mix thoroughly. Stir into the skillet until thickened.

*Yield: 6 diet servings*
*Calories per serving: 257*

## *INDONESIAN BEEF WITH ONIONS MENU PLAN*

*889 Calories (plus 200-calorie snack)*

Coffee, tea, or noncaloric beverages as desired

### BREAKFAST

1 egg, any style (use nonstick pan to scramble
    or fry)
1 frozen waffle
1 tablespoon diet maple syrup
1 tablespoon diet margarine

(*Substitute:* Basic Breakfast 2)

### LUNCH

1 cup low-fat cottage cheese
1 carrot, chopped
2 or 3 radishes, chopped
½ zucchini, chopped
½ tomato, chopped
3 rice cakes

(*Substitute:* Basic Lunch 2)

### DINNER

1 diet serving Indonesian Beef with Onions
½ serving any Super Salad
1 small orange
1 cup skim milk

## *Vitello Tonnato*

This elegant company dish is traditionally served cold. Here we suggest serving it hot on a bed of pasta and peas.

> 9 ounces lean veal loin, cut into 6 thin scallops
> 3 tablespoons whipped butter *or* diet margarine
> 1 tablespoon flour
> ⅓ cup canned condensed chicken broth, diluted with ⅓ cup water
> 2 medium onions, finely chopped
> 3 ounces water-packed white tuna, drained and flaked
> 2 tablespoons diet mayonnaise
> 1 tablespoon wine vinegar
> 1 tablespoon capers
> Salt and pepper to taste
> 6 ounces vermicelli or thin spaghetti
> 1 package frozen peas

Put the veal cutlets between two layers of wax paper and pound until very thin.

Melt 1 tablespoon butter in a large nonstick skillet. Brown the cutlets on both sides over moderate heat. This should cook them through if they are thin enough. Do not overcook because that tends to toughen the meat.

Remove the veal to a serving platter and keep it warm.

Melt 1 tablespoon butter in a small saucepan and blend in the flour. Add the broth slowly, stirring, and cook until it is smooth and begins to thicken. Remove from the heat and reserve.

Melt the remaining butter in a small nonstick skillet. Add the onions and sauté, stirring, until soft. Add the tuna, mayonnaise, vinegar, and half the capers, chopped. Simmer 5 minutes over very low heat. Taste, correct seasoning with salt and pepper, and add the mixture to the broth.

Simmer the sauce an additional 5 minutes. Place in a blender and purée.

Spoon the sauce over the veal and sprinkle with the remaining whole capers. Keep warm.

Cook the pasta and peas. Drain and combine. Serve with the veal and sauce.

*Yield: 6 diet servings*
*Calories per serving: 286*

---

## VITELLO TONNATO MENU PLAN

*905 Calories (plus 200-calorie snack)*
Coffee, tea, or noncaloric beverages as desired

**BREAKFAST**    (*Substitute:* Basic Breakfast 2)

1 egg, any style (use nonstick skillet to fry or scramble)
1 frozen waffle
1 tablespoon diet margarine
1 tablespoon diet maple syrup

**LUNCH**    (*Substitute:* Basic Lunch 3)

Cheese Tacos
    2 taco shells
    2 ounces Lite-line cheese
    1 tomato, chopped
    ½ small onion, chopped
    1 cup alfalfa sprouts
    Hot sauce (salsa)
1 cup skim milk

**DINNER**

1 diet serving Vitello Tonnato
1 small orange
1 cup skim milk

## Swiss Veal

You can find this dish on the menus of most fine restaurants in Switzerland under the name *geschnetzelte kalbsfleish*. It has lost nothing in translation, and its ease of preparation will delight you.

> 2 tablespoons whipped butter *or* diet margarine
> 2 large onions, diced
> 1 pound mushrooms, sliced
> 2 tablespoons chopped parsley
> ¼ teaspoon salt
> ½ teaspoon nutmeg
> 1½ tablespoons flour
> ½ pound lean veal cutlets, cut into thin strips
> ½ cup dry white wine
> ¼ cup evaporated low-fat milk
> 10 ounces dry spaetzle *or* egg noodles, cooked and
>   kept warm
> Salt and freshly ground black pepper to taste

Melt 1 tablespoon of butter in a large nonstick skillet. Add the onions and sauté, stirring, until soft. Add the remaining butter, the mushrooms, parsley, salt, and nutmeg and mix. Sauté, stirring, 2 minutes; cover and simmer 2 minutes longer to extract the mushroom juices. Uncover, sprinkle with the flour, and blend thoroughly.

Add the meat and increase the heat to high. Cook 3 minutes, stirring constantly. Reduce the heat and continue stirring 2 minutes longer.

Blend in the wine and milk, cover, and simmer over low heat 30 minutes or until the meat is tender.

Correct seasoning with salt and pepper and serve over the spaetzle.

*Yield: 6 diet servings*
*Calories per serving: 330*

## SWISS VEAL MENU PLAN
*895 Calories (plus 200-calorie snack)*

Coffee, tea, or noncaloric beverages as desired

### BREAKFAST

½ cantaloupe
½ cup low-fat cottage cheese
1 slice whole wheat bread

(*Substitute:* Basic Breakfast 1)

### LUNCH

Turkey Pocket
  2 ounces turkey
  ½ cucumber, chopped
  1 scallion, chopped (optional)
  1 teaspoon fresh dill *or* ½ teaspoon dried
  1 tablespoon diet mayonnaise
  1 1-ounce whole wheat bread pocket
1 cup skim milk

(*Substitute:* Basic Lunch 3)

### DINNER

1 diet serving Swiss Veal
1 serving Super Spinach Salad
½ cup skim milk

&*There's no law that says a family
can't eat the same food two days in
a row.*

# Bows with Eggplant

Though this recipe may seem to require more effort than some of the others, the result is well worth it. See if you don't agree.

1 pound eggplant
10 ounces medium-sized pasta bow ties
1 tablespoon olive oil
1 clove garlic, crushed
1 small chili pepper (optional)
3 ounces fresh broccoli, broken into tiny flowerets, blanched and drained
6 ounces lean veal, ground
2 tablespoons chopped parsley
½ teaspoon coarse salt
¼ teaspoon freshly ground black pepper

Prick the eggplant all over with a fork and bake in a pre-heated 400°F oven for 30 minutes or until it is cooked through. Set aside.

Cook the pasta, drain, and keep warm.

Cut the eggplant in half and scoop out the flesh. Discard the shell and chop or mash the flesh. Set aside.

Heat the oil in a large nonstick skillet; add the garlic and chili pepper and cook, stirring, until the garlic begins to brown. Discard both the garlic and pepper and add the broccoli. Cook, stirring, 30 seconds. Remove the skillet from the stove. Using a slotted spoon, transfer the broccoli to a bowl and keep it warm.

Return the skillet to the stove, add the veal, and brown quickly, stirring continuously. Stir in the eggplant, sprinkle with the parsley, and cook, stirring, 3 minutes.

Top the warm pasta with the hot eggplant and toss. Sprinkle with the hot broccoli, salt, and pepper; toss again and serve immediately.

*Yield: 6 diet servings*
*Calories per serving: 262*

## BOWS WITH EGGPLANT MENU PLAN

*907 Calories (plus 200-calorie snack)*

Coffee, tea, or noncaloric beverages as desired

### BREAKFAST

½ cup unsweetened pineapple chunks
½ cup low-fat cottage cheese
1 slice raisin bread toast

(*Substitute:* Basic Breakfast 1)

### LUNCH

1 toasted bagel
2 slices Lite-line cheese
½ cup skim milk

(*Substitute:* Basic Lunch 3)

### DINNER

1 diet serving Bows with Eggplant
1 serving any Super Salad
½ cup skim milk

⋖§ *You'll never stick to an exercise schedule if it's inconvenient, unpleasant, or incompatible with your work or family routine. Do something that can easily be incorporated into your lifestyle.*

## Honeymoon Casserole

In some areas of the Middle East, this casserole is traditionally served to honeymooners for breakfast. It makes an even
better dinner dish. You may freeze it right in the casserole
before cooking. Bring it back to room temperature and bake
it according to the directions in the recipe.

    Nonstick vegetable oil spray
    12 ounces very lean leg of lamb, ground
    2 medium onions, finely chopped
    2 cloves garlic, minced
    1 cup finely chopped celery
    1 teaspoon salt
    ½ teaspoon sugar
    1 teaspoon dried bell pepper flakes
    1 teaspoon dried or fresh mint
    1 package or 1 teaspoon instant powdered chicken
       broth
    ¼ pound fresh mushrooms, finely chopped
    1 can condensed tomato soup, diluted with ¼ cup
       water
    6 ounces thin egg noodles, cooked and drained
    1 ounce Parmesan cheese, grated
    ½ teaspoon paprika

Prepare a shallow baking dish or casserole by spraying the
bottom and sides lightly with nonstick vegetable oil. Set
aside.

Brown the meat in a medium-sized nonstick skillet over
moderate heat. Add the onions, garlic, and celery. Sauté, stirring. Drain off any fat that may collect.

Stir in the salt, sugar, pepper flakes, mint, broth, mushrooms, and soup. Simmer gently 20 minutes, stirring occasionally to prevent sticking.

Place half the noodles on the bottom of the casserole.

Cover with the cooked meat mixture, followed by the second half of the noodles, and finish with the remaining meat.

Combine the cheese and paprika in a small bowl. Mix thoroughly and sprinkle over the meat.

Bake 30 minutes in a preheated 350°F oven.

*Yield: 6 diet servings*
*Calories per serving: 289*

---

### HONEYMOON CASSEROLE MENU PLAN

*907 Calories (plus 200-calorie snack)*

**Coffee, tea, or noncaloric beverages as desired**

**BREAKFAST**  (*Substitute:* Basic Breakfast 3)

½ grapefruit
½ bagel, toasted
1 slice skim-milk mozzarella cheese

**LUNCH**  (*Substitute:* Basic Lunch 1)

Deli Pocket
  4 ounces lean corned beef
  1 1-ounce whole wheat bread pocket
1 dill pickle
½ cup skim milk

**DINNER**

1 diet serving Honeymoon Casserole
½ cup cooked carrots
½ serving any Super Salad
1 cup skim milk

## *Ionian Stew*

This Greek dish is typical of the part of the world where lamb rather than beef is raised. You'll like the pleasant combination of spices and herbs that lend an enticing fragrance to what is also a delicious combination of flavors.

This stew tastes best hot.

> 1 tablespoon olive oil
> 6 ounces very lean leg of lamb, cut into ½-inch cubes
> 3 medium onions, sliced
> 8 ounces canned tomato sauce
> 2 tablespoons water
> ½ teaspoon salt
> ½ teaspoon marjoram
> ⅛ teaspoon freshly ground black pepper
> 2 cloves, whole
> 1 medium eggplant, cut into ½-inch cubes
> 2 green peppers, seeded and coarsely diced
> 1 package frozen okra, partially thawed and sliced (optional)
> 3 medium tomatoes, peeled, seeded, and quartered
> 6 ounces Superoni elbow macaroni
> 1 tablespoon chopped parsley

Heat the oil in a 3-quart saucepan and brown the lamb on all sides. Add the onions and sauté gently, stirring, 5 minutes. Combine the tomato sauce, water, salt, marjoram, pepper, and cloves in a bowl. Add the mixture to the saucepan, cover, and simmer 30 minutes.

Mix the eggplant, peppers, and okra and add to the lamb; cover and simmer an additional 20 minutes or until the meat is tender. Remove the cloves.

Add the tomatoes and cook, uncovered, 10 minutes longer. If the sauce is too thin, increase the heat and cook, stirring occasionally, until it thickens to your taste.

Prepare the macaroni, drain, and transfer to a decorative serving bowl. Pour the stew over the pasta and sprinkle with parsley.

*Yield: 6 diet servings*
*Calories per serving: 247*

---

### IONIAN STEW MENU PLAN

*906 Calories (plus 200-calorie snack)*
Coffee, tea, or noncaloric beverages as desired

#### BREAKFAST

1 egg, boiled, or cooked in nonstick pan
1 sausage link
1 slice whole wheat toast
½ cup skim milk

(*Substitute:* Basic Breakfast 4)

#### LUNCH

½ cup low-fat cottage cheese
1 tablespoon chopped parsley
1 tablespoon fresh or dried dill
½ cucumber
1 bran muffin, toasted
½ cup skim milk

(*Substitute:* Basic Lunch 2)

#### DINNER

1 diet serving Ionian Stew
1 serving Basic Super Salad
1 cup skim milk

---

## *Swedish Lamb*

Swedish Lamb may be frozen in individual diet portions and reheated slowly when desired. If you freeze this dish, don't cook the pasta in advance. One diet serving of pasta for this dish is 1⅓ ounces uncooked Superoni fettuccine.

8 ounces very lean leg of lamb, cut into small cubes
⅛ teaspoon salt
Generous pinch freshly ground black pepper
1 tablespoon sunflower *or* safflower oil
1 onion, chopped
¼ cup unsweetened apple juice
1 beef bouillon cube, dissolved in ½ cup boiling water
2 teaspoons tomato paste
2 medium Granny Smith or other tart apples, peeled, cored, and diced
8 ounces Superoni fettuccine
2 teaspoons lemon juice
Generous pinch cinnamon
½ teaspoon dried or fresh chopped dill
½ teaspoon ground cloves
2 teaspoons brown sugar

Sprinkle the lamb cubes with salt and pepper. Reserve.

Heat the oil in a medium-sized nonstick skillet and add the onion. Sauté until soft. Add the lamb and stir.

Bring the apple juice to a boil in a small saucepan. Pour it over the lamb and simmer over very low heat until almost all the juice is cooked out — about 15 minutes.

Combine the bouillon and tomato paste and stir until thoroughly blended. Add the broth mixture and apples to the skillet, cover, and simmer about 20 minutes or until the meat is tender.

Meanwhile, cook the pasta, drain, and keep warm.

When the meat is tender, stir in the lemon juice, cinnamon, dill, cloves, and sugar. Cover and simmer 5 minutes.

Serve the meat and apples over the pasta.

*Yield: 6 diet servings*
*Calories per serving: 277*

---

### SWEDISH LAMB MENU PLAN

*901 Calories (plus 200-calorie snack)*

Coffee, tea, or noncaloric beverages as desired

**BREAKFAST**

   1 slice rye toast
   1 slice cooked lean ham
   1 slice Swiss cheese, melted on top

   (*Substitute:* Basic Breakfast 4)

**LUNCH**

   Vegetable Dip
      1 cup plain low-fat yogurt, seasoned with
      1 tablespoon dry onion soup mix
      1 green pepper, cut in strips
      1 carrot, cut in sticks
      ½ cup shredded red cabbage
      1 cucumber, cut in spears
      6 radishes (optional)
   1 1-ounce whole wheat bread pocket

   (*Substitute:* Basic Lunch 2)

**DINNER**

   1 diet serving Swedish Lamb
   1 cup skim milk
   ½ cantaloupe *or* 1 orange

## Shells with Tuna Sauce

This one-dish dinner is just as good cold as it is hot and it keeps well in the refrigerator for two or three days. Or divide it into individual servings and freeze it. Reheat the frozen dish slowly.

10 ounces small pasta shells
1 tablespoon olive oil
1 clove garlic, minced or put through a garlic press
1 medium onion, sliced very thin
½ teaspoon coarse salt
¼ teaspoon sugar
½ teaspoon dried oregano
1 cup canned peeled ground tomatoes
1 medium fresh tomato, seeded and chopped coarsely
1 tablespoon capers *or* chopped dill pickle
3½ ounces water-packed white tuna, drained and mashed with a fork
¼ cup chopped flat leaf parsley

Cook the pasta until tender but not soft and drain. Keep the pasta warm while you prepare the sauce.

Heat the oil in a 1-quart saucepan. Add the garlic and onions and sprinkle with salt and sugar. Sauté, stirring, until the onions are soft. Do not brown.

Sprinkle with the oregano and stir in the ground tomatoes, chopped tomato, and capers. Reduce the heat and cook, stirring, about 4 minutes.

Add the tuna, stir to mix, and cook 2 minutes longer.

Drain the pasta thoroughly. Add the sauce and toss. Sprinkle with parsley and toss again.

Serve immediately.

*Yield: 4 diet servings*
*Calories per serving: 374*

## *SHELLS WITH TUNA SAUCE MENU PLAN*

*905 calories (plus 200-calorie snack)*

Coffee, tea, or noncaloric beverages as desired

### BREAKFAST

½ cup orange juice
½ cup hot cereal
1 cup skim milk

(*Substitute:* Basic Breakfast 1)

### LUNCH

Cucumber Boats
1 large cucumber, halved and seeded
1 cup low-fat cottage cheese, mixed with
1 tablespoon dry onion soup mix
1 scallion, chopped (optional)
½ cup chopped green pepper
1 tablespoon chopped parsley
1 English Muffin, toasted

(*Substitute:* Basic Lunch 2)

### DINNER

1 diet serving Shells with Tuna Sauce

*❧ If you spent as much time exercising
as you do finding excuses for not
having the time, you'd be a lot thinner.*

## *Tangy Tuna-Macaroni Salad*

Although we suggest this recipe as a salad, it's just as good served as a hot entrée. Simply toss the broccoli and pasta together while they're still warm, add the tuna dressing, and toss gently again. Sprinkle the top with chopped parsley or chopped dill and you have a beautiful as well as delicious carbohydrate-rich dish with which to enjoy your diet.

1 7-ounce can water-packed white tuna, drained
   and mashed
3 tablespoons diet mayonnaise
2 teaspoons cider *or* distilled vinegar
¼ cup low-fat cottage cheese
2 teaspoons Worcestershire sauce
1 tablespoon lemon juice
2 tablespoons ketchup
1 teaspoon sugar
1 teaspoon garlic salt *or* ½ teaspoon garlic powder
Pinch dried tarragon
½ teaspoon Dijon mustard
¼ cup low-fat evaporated milk
4 cups fresh broccoli, broken into tiny flowerets,
   cooked until just tender, and chilled
10 ounces Superoni elbow macaroni, cooked,
   drained, and chilled
Chopped parsley *or* dill for garnish

Combine the tuna, mayonnaise, vinegar, cottage cheese, Worcestershire, lemon juice, ketchup, sugar, garlic, tarragon, and mustard in a blender jar or food processor fitted with a metal blade. Process 1 minute. Add the milk and process until smooth. Chill until needed.

Before serving, combine the broccoli and macaroni in a large serving bowl and toss. Add the tuna dressing and toss again. Sprinkle with parsley or dill and serve on a bed of lettuce.

*Yield: 6 diet servings*
*Calories per serving: 264*

---

### *TANGY TUNA-MACARONI SALAD MENU PLAN*

*905 Calories (plus 200-calorie snack)*
Coffee, tea, or noncaloric beverages as desired

### BREAKFAST

1 egg, any style (use nonstick pan to scramble
  or fry)
1 slice Canadian bacon, broiled
1 slice rye toast

(*Substitute:* Basic Breakfast 4)

### LUNCH

Asparagus-Cheese Melt
  1 English muffin, topped with
  4 spears fresh or frozen asparagus and
  2 ounces Lite-line cheese
    Melt under broiler.
1 carrot

(*Substitute:* Basic Lunch 4)

### DINNER

1 diet serving Tangy Tuna-Macaroni Salad
1 cup fresh or unsweetened frozen strawberries
  *or* 1 orange
1 cup skim milk

## *Sweet Pepper Spaghetti*

No fish ever had better company than this sweet pepper sauce. This recipe yields generous diet portions, so you needn't feel uncomfortable serving it to nondieters.

> 1 slice lemon
> 1 teaspoon freshly squeezed lemon juice
> 1 cup water
> 6 ounces cod, cusk, tilefish, or other firm, lean fish fillet
> 4 large red bell peppers, finely chopped
> 2 small shallots, finely minced
> 2 tablespoons chopped parsley
> 1 tablespoon olive oil
> ¼ cup water
> Generous pinch salt
> 1 tablespoon red wine vinegar
> 1 teaspoon sugar
> 8 ounces Superoni spaghetti
> Freshly ground black pepper to taste

Combine the lemon, lemon juice, and water in a small skillet. Bring to a boil, reduce the heat, and simmer 1 minute. Add the fish, cover, and poach 10 to 12 minutes or until cooked through. It should flake easily when pricked with a fork. Set aside and allow to cool in poaching liquid.

Combine the peppers, shallots, parsley, oil, water, and salt in a medium-sized heavy-bottomed saucepan. Bring to a boil, cover, and reduce the heat to low. Simmer slowly for 25 minutes. Check periodically to see if more water is necessary. Add small amounts as needed.

When the peppers are tender, add the vinegar and sugar. Cover and simmer 5 minutes longer.

Meanwhile, remove the fish from its court bouillon with a slotted spoon and drain thoroughly. Gently separate it into flakes.

Cook the spaghetti and drain. Transfer to a serving bowl. Gently fold the fish flakes into the sauce, correct seasoning, and pour over the spaghetti. Sprinkle with pepper. Serve immediately.

*Yield: 4 diet servings*
*Calories per serving: 299*

---

### SWEET PEPPER SPAGHETTI MENU PLAN
*894 Calories (plus 200-calorie snack)*

Coffee, tea, or noncaloric beverages as desired

### BREAKFAST

½ grapefruit
½ bagel, toasted
1 slice skim-milk mozzarella cheese

(*Substitute:* Basic Breakfast 3)

### LUNCH

Deli Pocket
  4 ounces lean corned beef
  1 1-ounce whole wheat bread pocket
1 dill pickle
½ cup skim milk

(*Substitute:* Basic Lunch 1)

### DINNER

1 diet serving Sweet Pepper Spaghetti
½ serving Super Spinach Salad
1 cup skim milk

# Seafood Suprême

Seafood lovers take note: if this is dieting, you'll never want to stop. However, don't try to freeze this dish. Save it for an occasion when enough people will be around to finish it.

> 1 tablespoon olive oil
> 4 scallions, white and green parts, trimmed and finely chopped
> ½ pound mushrooms, scrubbed, trimmed, and thinly sliced
> 2 tablespoons instant flour
> 1 cup hot low-fat milk
> ½ cup clam juice
> 4 tablespoons dry sherry
> Generous pinch dry mustard *and* curry powder
> Salt, pepper, and cayenne to taste
> 2 tablespoons finely chopped parsley
> 2 egg yolks, slightly beaten
> 2 tablespoons freshly squeezed lemon juice
> 6 ounces crab meat, picked over carefully
> 4 ounces cooked shrimp, cut in half
> 18 medium-sized fresh shucked oysters
> 6 ounces noodles, cooked and kept warm
> Chopped parsley for garnish

Heat the oil in a large stainless-steel or nonstick skillet, and sauté the scallions and mushrooms until soft and moist. Sprinkle the flour over the mixture and blend thoroughly. Cook, stirring constantly, about 2 minutes.

Combine the milk, clam juice, sherry, mustard, curry, salt, pepper, cayenne, and parsley in a small bowl and mix thoroughly. Add the liquid very gradually to the skillet, stirring constantly, and cook 2 minutes. Stir a little of the hot sauce into the yolks, then stir the yolks into the sauce.

Using a wooden spoon, carefully blend in the lemon juice,

crab, shrimp, and oysters. Cook only until the oysters curl. Serve immediately over the cooked noodles and garnish with parsley.

*Yield: 6 diet servings*
*Calories per serving: 268*

---

### SEAFOOD SUPRÊME MENU PLAN

*905 Calories (plus 200-calorie snack)*

Coffee, tea, or noncaloric beverages as desired

#### BREAKFAST

½ cup orange juice
½ cup cooked cereal
1 cup skim milk

(*Substitute:* Basic Breakfast 1)

#### LUNCH

Chicken in the Corn
   2½ ounces cooked chicken
   1 corn muffin, toasted
   ½ cup skim milk

(*Substitute:* Basic Lunch 1)

#### DINNER

1 diet serving Seafood Suprême
1 serving Basic Super Salad
½ cup skim milk

# 6

## Rice

### Chicken in Red Wine

While this casserole should not be frozen, it may be baked ahead and reheated in a preheated 375°F oven for 10 minutes (or until heated through) at serving time.

>  Nonstick vegetable oil spray
>  8 chicken thighs (about 1¾ pounds), skin and all visible fat removed
>  1 tablespoon olive oil
>  2 medium onions, chopped
>  ½ pound mushrooms, scrubbed, trimmed, and sliced
>  1 cup dry red wine, preferably Burgundy
>  2 cups cooked white rice
>  1-pound package frozen peas
>  1 cup shredded Boston or other lettuce
>  ¼ teaspoon savory
>  2 canned pimientos, cut into thin strips
>  Salt and freshly ground pepper to taste

Prepare a medium-sized casserole by spraying the bottom and sides with nonstick vegetable oil. Set aside.

Prick the chicken all over and broil on all sides until brown. Transfer to the prepared casserole and keep warm.

Heat the oil in a nonstick skillet. Add the onions and mushrooms and sauté until soft. Add to the casserole.

Pour the wine over the chicken, cover, and bake 35 minutes in a preheated 325°F oven.

Toss together the rice, peas, lettuce, savory, and pimientos in a large bowl. When the chicken is fork tender, add the rice mixture to the casserole. Correct seasoning and return the casserole, covered, to the oven. Bake an additional 15 minutes or until the peas are tender but not overcooked.

*Yield: 6 diet servings*
*Calories per serving: 377*

---

### CHICKEN IN RED WINE MENU PLAN

*894 Calories (plus 200-calorie snack)*

Coffee, tea, or noncaloric beverages as desired

**BREAKFAST**

1 medium egg, scrambled in nonstick pan
1 slice skim-milk mozzarella cheese
1 slice whole wheat toast

(*Substitute:* Basic Breakfast 2)

**LUNCH**

½ cup low-fat cottage cheese
1 tablespoon chopped parsley
1 tablespoon fresh or dried dill
½ cucumber
1 bran muffin, toasted
½ cup skim milk

(*Substitute:* Basic Lunch 1)

**DINNER**

1 diet serving Chicken in Red Wine
1 serving Basic Super Salad
½ cup skim milk

## *Chicken Sausage and Rice*

This dish makes a great outdoor barbecue dinner. Follow the directions for the rice and keep it warm in the top part of a double boiler, which can be placed right on the barbecue grill.

Prepare the skewers and brown the food over hot coals. You'll get rave notices.

2 green peppers, stems and seeds removed
1 large tomato, cut into 3 wedges and seeded
2 medium boiling onions
6 chicken frankfurters
2 teaspoons cider vinegar
1 package frozen peas, cooked
Pinch dried ground marjoram
½ teaspoon sugar
1 tablespoon whipped butter *or* diet margarine
¼ teaspoon salt
3 cups cooked white rice, kept warm

Cut the peppers into 3 thick rings. Cut each ring into quarters and blanch 2 minutes. Drain and set aside.

Cut each tomato wedge in half to make 6 tomato triangles. Set aside.

Cut each onion into six wedges and blanch 2 minutes. Set aside.

Cook the frankfurters in a saucepan in just enough water to cover. Add the vinegar, mix, and bring to a boil. Reduce the heat and simmer gently for 10 minutes. Drain and cut each frankfurter into thirds.

Thread the meat and vegetables on six metal or bamboo skewers in the following order: onion, pepper, frankfurter, pepper, frankfurter, pepper, tomato, pepper, frankfurter, onion.

Sprinkle the hot peas with marjoram and sugar. Toss. Add

the butter and toss gently until it melts. Add to the rice, sprinkle with salt, and mix. Keep warm.

Brown the prepared skewers under a preheated broiler and serve over the rice mixture.

*Yield: 6 diet servings*
*Calories per serving: 255*

---

### CHICKEN SAUSAGE AND RICE MENU PLAN

*889 Calories (plus 200-calorie snack)*

Coffee, tea, or noncaloric beverages as desired

**BREAKFAST**

1 bran muffin
½ cup low-fat cottage cheese
1 tablespoon diet jelly

(*Substitute:* Basic Breakfast 1)

**LUNCH**

Greek Tuna Pocket
2 ounces water-packed tuna
1 ounce feta cheese
1 1-ounce whole wheat bread pocket
½ cup skim milk

(*Substitute:* Basic Lunch 1)

**DINNER**

1 diet serving Chicken Sausage and Rice
2 stalks broccoli
½ serving any Super Salad
1 cup skim milk

## *Five-Spice Chicken and Rice*

Cook the chicken ahead if you wish, but prepare the rice just before you are ready to serve the dish.

> ½ tablespoon sesame oil
> ½ tablespoon vegetable oil
> 2 tablespoons sugar
> 4 tablespoons soy sauce
> 2 tablespoons dry sherry
> 1 teaspoon grated ginger
> ½ clove garlic, grated
> ½ teaspoon 5-spice powder (may be purchased anywhere oriental products are sold, *or* combine equal amounts of cinnamon, mace, allspice, nutmeg, and ground aniseed)
> ⅛ teaspoon salt
> 4 cubes chicken bouillon, dissolved in 3 cups boiling water
> 1 cup brown rice
> 5 scallions, trimmed, green and white parts chopped separately
> 6 small chicken thighs (10 ounces total), skinned
> 2 tablespoons chopped fresh coriander

Combine the sesame oil, vegetable oil, sugar, soy sauce, sherry, ginger, garlic, five-spice powder, and salt in a skillet just large enough to hold the chicken in one layer. Stir to mix thoroughly until the sugar and salt dissolve. Bring to a boil; reduce the heat and simmer gently 2 minutes.

Meanwhile, bring the bouillon to a rolling boil in a large saucepan and add the rice and white part of the scallions. Cover and set the heat to low. Cook until the rice is tender.

While the rice is cooking, add the chicken thighs to the sauce in the skillet, cover, and simmer over low heat 15 minutes on each side. Remove from the heat, sprinkle with coriander, and set aside.

Add the green parts of the scallions to the rice and toss.

Serve the chicken over the rice and pass the sauce.

*Yield: 4 diet servings*
*Calories per serving: 306*

---

### *FIVE-SPICE CHICKEN AND RICE MENU PLAN*

*900 Calories (plus 200-calorie snack)*

Coffee, tea, or noncaloric beverages as desired

## BREAKFAST

⅓ cantaloupe *or* ½ grapefruit
½ cup low-fat cottage cheese
½ whole wheat English muffin

(*Substitute:* Basic Breakfast 1)

## LUNCH

Tostada Melt
2 frozen corn tortillas, heated in nonstick
pan
2 ounces water-packed tuna
½ tomato, sliced
1 ounce skim-milk mozzarella cheese
Melt under broiler.
½ green pepper, cut in strips
½ cup skim milk

(*Substitute:* Basic Lunch 1)

## DINNER

1 diet serving Five-Spice Chicken and Rice
½ cup fresh or unsweetened frozen strawberries

## *Jambalaya*

This hearty Creole dish provides a surprisingly generous treat for dieters and nondieters alike.

Bake the casserole ahead, if you like, and reheat it at serving time in a preheated 375°F oven for 10 to 15 minutes.

>  Nonstick vegetable oil spray
>  8 ounces cooked diced frozen (thawed) or leftover chicken
>  2 16-ounce cans stewed tomatoes
>  1 package frozen sliced okra, slightly defrosted
>  1 cup diced celery
>  3 cups cooked rice
>  ½ cup minced onions
>  1 cup minced green bell peppers
>  2 teaspoons coarse salt
>  ¼ teaspoon freshly ground black pepper
>  2 teaspoons chili powder
>  ½ cup dry white wine
>  Tabasco sauce (optional)
>  3 tablespoons dry bread crumbs, mixed with
>  2 ounces skim-milk mozzarella cheese, grated

Spray the bottom and sides of a 4-quart casserole for which you have a cover with nonstick vegetable oil and set aside.

Put the chicken in a large saucepan.

Drain the tomatoes and reserve ¼ cup of their liquid. Add both the tomatoes and the reserved liquid to the chicken.

Add the remaining ingredients, except the bread crumbs, cheese, and Tabasco sauce, and stir gently to mix.

Bring the Jambalaya to a boil over high heat, then reduce the heat, cover, and simmer 20 minutes, stirring occasionally. Take care that the mix does not stick to the bottom and burn. Taste; add a few drops of Tabasco sauce if you desire.

Turn the mix into the prepared casserole, smooth the

top with a rubber spatula, and sprinkle with the bread crumb/cheese mix.

Cover and bake 15 minutes in a preheated 350°F oven. Remove the cover and bake 15 minutes to brown.

*Yield: 6 diet servings*
*Calories per serving: 236*

---

### JAMBALAYA MENU PLAN

*873 Calories (plus 200-calorie snack)*

Coffee, tea, or noncaloric beverages as desired

**BREAKFAST**   (*Substitute:* Basic Breakfast 1)

½ cup grapefruit juice
1 cup Cheerios
1 cup skim milk

**LUNCH**   (*Substitute:* Basic Lunch 1)

Deli Pocket
  4 ounces lean corned beef
  1 1-ounce whole wheat bread pocket
½ serving Super Coleslaw
1 dill pickle
½ cup skim milk

**DINNER**

1 diet serving Jambalaya
½ serving Super Coleslaw
1 ounce French bread
1 teaspoon diet margarine
½ cup skim milk

## Spiced Chicken

If you don't insist on your food "steaming" on your plate, try preparing this dish ahead and serving it at room temperature.

> 1 cup brown rice
> 3 cups boiling water
> 6 small chicken thighs, skin and all visible fat removed
> 1 teaspoon freshly squeezed lemon juice
> 1 teaspoon garlic salt
> ½ teaspoon paprika
> 2 teaspoons fresh or dried chopped dill
> ½ teaspoon salt
> 1 package frozen baby lima beans, partially thawed
> 2 tablespoons whipped butter *or* diet margarine

Add the rice to the boiling water; cover, reduce the heat, and simmer until the rice is soft.

Meanwhile, pat the chicken thighs dry, then moisten slightly with the lemon juice. Combine the garlic and paprika and rub into the thighs.

Broil the thighs on both sides under a hot, preheated broiler until done. Remove and keep warm.

When the rice is tender, add the dill, salt, beans, and butter; cover and simmer 10 minutes or until the beans are tender. Add water if necessary to avoid burning.

Drain the excess liquid and serve accompanied by the chicken.

> *Yield: 6 diet servings*
> *Calories per serving: 252*

## SPICED CHICKEN MENU PLAN

*882 Calories (plus 200-calorie snack)*

Coffee, tea, or noncaloric beverages as desired

### BREAKFAST

1 poached egg
1 slice cooked lean ham
1 slice whole wheat toast

(*Substitute:* Basic Breakfast 4)

### LUNCH

Banana Split
   1 cup low-fat cottage cheese, mixed with
   1 teaspoon cinnamon sugar
   1 banana, sliced
1 1-ounce whole wheat bread pocket, toasted

(*Substitute:* Basic Lunch 2)

### DINNER

1 diet serving Spiced Chicken
1 serving Super Coleslaw
1 cup skim milk

*≈§ Are you addicted to a particular
food? Don't choose it for your daily
snack. It will be as safe in your
house as chickens in a coop when
the fox comes in.*

## Chicken-Rice Pilau

If you want to freeze this casserole, bake it first and let it cool completely. To serve, thaw it in the refrigerator and reheat it in a preheated 375 °F oven for about 10 minutes.

Nonstick vegetable oil spray
¼ cup dried currants
3 scallions, trimmed and finely chopped
1 teaspoon salt
¼ teaspoon freshly ground black pepper
½ teaspoon ground mace
1 cup canned condensed beef consommé
½ cup water
1 tablespoon whipped butter *or* diet margarine
⅓ cup fine bread crumbs
2 cups frozen (thawed) cooked diced *or* leftover chicken, divided into 2 portions
3 cups cooked brown rice, divided into 2 portions
3 medium, ripe tomatoes, finely chopped

Prepare a medium casserole or baking dish by spraying the bottom and sides with nonstick vegetable oil. Set aside.

Prepare the seasoning mix in a small bowl by combining the currants, scallions, salt, pepper, and mace. Mix well and reserve.

Combine the consommé and water in a small saucepan. Bring to a boil, remove from the heat, and reserve.

Melt the butter in a small nonstick skillet. Add the bread crumbs and stir to mix. Remove from the heat and reserve.

To assemble the pilau, arrange half the chicken in the prepared casserole and sprinkle with a little seasoning mix. Cover with half the rice. Sprinkle with a little seasoning mix. Top the rice with half the tomatoes and a little seasoning mix. Repeat the layers.

Pour in the consommé, top with the buttered bread crumbs and bake, uncovered, 30 minutes or until brown in a preheated 375 °F oven.

*Yield: 4 diet servings*
*Calories per serving: 358*

---

### CHICKEN-RICE PILAU MENU PLAN
*901 Calories (plus 200-calorie snack)*
**Coffee, tea, or noncaloric beverages as desired**

**BREAKFAST**

 1 frozen waffle, spread with
 ¼ cup low-fat cottage cheese, sprinkled with
 1 tablespoon wheat germ, mixed with
 1 teaspoon cinnamon sugar
 ½ banana

 (*Substitute:* Basic Breakfast 1)

**LUNCH**

 Tostada with Cheese
  2 frozen corn tortillas, heated in nonstick
   pan
  2 ounces Lite-line cheese, shredded
  ½ green pepper, chopped
  ½ medium tomato, chopped
  Salsa to taste
 1 cup skim milk

 (*Substitute:* Basic Lunch 3)

**DINNER**

 1 diet serving Chicken-Rice Pilau
 ½ serving any Super Salad
 ½ cup skim milk

---

## Paella Valenciana

This traditional Spanish peasant dish is a lovely blend of rice, chicken, vegetables, and seafood. The rice slowly absorbs the exquisite color and flavor of the saffron, which makes this an attractive, delicious, yet deceptively easy meal.

Paella does not keep well as a leftover, so you may want to cut the recipe in half. Half a recipe produces one diet portion and one generous regular portion.

> 6 small chicken drumsticks
> 1 tablespoon olive oil
> 3 cloves garlic, finely chopped
> 4 medium onions, chopped
> 1 cup brown rice
> 1 cup canned chicken broth
> 1½ cups bottled clam juice
> 2 teaspoons freshly squeezed lemon juice
> 1 ounce pepperoni, thinly sliced and each slice cut in half
> ¼ pound cod fillet, cut into 6 pieces
> 3 to 4 strands Spanish saffron
> Salt and pepper to taste
> 14 large clams, scrubbed very well
> 12 medium shrimp (about 10 ounces), shelled and deveined but tails left intact
> 1 small can pimientos, cut into strips

Brown the chicken quickly all over under a hot broiler. Set aside.

Heat the oil in a large nonstick skillet for which you have a cover. Add the garlic and onions and sauté until just soft. Add the rice, broth, clam juice, and lemon juice, stir, and bring to a boil. Add the pepperoni, cod, saffron, salt, and pepper. Bring back to a boil, reduce the heat, and cover. Simmer 15 minutes.

Uncover, arrange the clams and shrimp on top of the rice.

Recover and simmer an additional 15 minutes or until the rice is cooked, the chicken tender, and the clams have opened. Discard any clam that has not opened.
Sprinkle the top with pimiento.

*Yield: 6 diet servings*
*Calories per serving: 314*

---

### PAELLA VALENCIANA MENU PLAN

*895 Calories (plus 200-calorie snack)*
Coffee, tea, or noncaloric beverages as desired

## BREAKFAST

½ banana, sliced, mixed with
½ cup low-fat cottage cheese, mixed with
¼ cup plain low-fat yogurt
2 Melba toast rounds

(*Substitute:* Basic Breakfast 4)

## LUNCH

Asparagus-Cheese Melt
1 English muffin, topped with
4 spears fresh or frozen asparagus
2 ounces Lite-line cheese
Melt under broiler.
1 carrot

(*Substitute:* Basic Lunch 3)

## DINNER

1 diet serving Paella Valenciana
½ serving any Super Salad
½ cup skim milk

## *Soused Chicken Livers*

This dish, elegant enough to serve to guests, is simple to prepare. You will make it again and again.

> 2 tablespoons flour
> ¼ teaspoon salt
> ⅛ teaspoon freshly ground black pepper
> 1 pound chicken livers, membranes removed, cut
>   into quarters
> 2 tablespoons whipped butter *or* diet margarine
> 2 scallions, white and green parts, chopped
> ¼ pound mushrooms, thinly sliced
> ¼ cup canned condensed chicken broth, diluted
>   with ¼ cup water
> 2 tablespoons Sour Half-and-Half (page 28)
> 2 tablespoons brandy
> ½ 10-ounce package frozen peas, cooked
> ¼ teaspoon dried savory
> 3 cups cooked white rice, kept warm

Combine the flour, salt, and pepper in a paper bag and shake. Add the chicken livers, shake to coat lightly, and remove. Reserve the flour remaining in the bag.

Melt 1 tablespoon butter in a medium-sized nonstick skillet. Add the scallions and mushrooms and sauté, stirring, until tender and the mushrooms have given up their liquid. Add the livers, increase the heat, and sauté them, stirring to prevent burning, until brown. Remove from the heat.

Melt the remaining butter in a small nonstick saucepan. Add the reserved flour and blend. Slowly stir in the chicken broth and half-and-half. Blend completely.

Return the livers to moderate heat, add the sauce, and simmer (do not boil) 3 minutes. Stir in the brandy and simmer an additional 3 minutes. Correct seasoning and keep warm.

Combine the peas and savory in a bowl. Add the rice and

toss. Transfer to a serving dish and top with the chicken livers and sauce.

*Yield: 6 diet servings*
*Calories per serving: 238*

---

### *SOUSED CHICKEN LIVERS MENU PLAN*

*898 Calories (plus 200-calorie snack)*
Coffee, tea, or noncaloric beverages as desired

**BREAKFAST**

　　1 frozen waffle, sprinkled with
　　1 teaspoon cinnamon sugar
　　½ cup vanilla-flavored low-fat yogurt
　　1 teaspoon raisins

　　(*Substitute:* Basic Breakfast 1)

**LUNCH**

　　Corn-Fed Tuna
　　　　3 ounces water-packed tuna
　　　　1 cucumber, chopped
　　　　1 tablespoon parsley, chopped
　　1 corn muffin, toasted
　　½ cup skim milk

　　(*Substitute:* Basic Lunch 1)

**DINNER**

　　1 diet serving Soused Chicken Livers
　　1 serving any Super Salad
　　1 cup skim milk

## Turkey Curry

Prepare this curry ahead for enhanced flavor. You may freeze it and reheat it slowly. The rice, however, should be prepared just before serving.

> 1 teaspoon turmeric
> ½ teaspoon salt
> 8 ounces turkey breast cutlets
> 1 tablespoon vegetable oil
> 2 medium onions, thinly sliced
> 2 cloves garlic, minced
> 1 tablespoon curry powder (less if you prefer)
> 1 teaspoon ground coriander
> 2 cloves, whole
> ⅛ teaspoon cinnamon
> 1 small can peeled tomatoes
> 1 bell pepper, seeded and cut into thin strips
> 1 can condensed cream of mushroom soup
> ¼ cup dry white wine
> 1 cup white rice
> ⅓ cup chopped fresh coriander

Combine the turmeric and salt in a plastic or paper bag and shake to mix. Cut the turkey into small pieces and add to the bag. Shake.

Heat the oil in a large nonstick skillet over moderate heat. Add the turkey and brown lightly. Remove the meat with a slotted spoon, and keep warm.

Place the onions and garlic in the skillet and brown lightly, stirring. Add the curry, coriander, cloves, and cinnamon and sauté, stirring frequently, about 2 minutes. Add the tomatoes, pepper, and turkey; stir in the soup and half the wine. Cover and simmer slowly 45 minutes, adding wine when necessary to keep moist.

Cook the rice and toss with the chopped fresh coriander.

Serve the curry over the rice.

*Yield: 6 diet servings*
*Calories per serving: 263*

---

### TURKEY CURRY MENU PLAN

*914 Calories (plus 200-calorie snack)*

Coffee, tea, or noncaloric beverages as desired

**BREAKFAST**

1 slice bread, dipped in
1 beaten egg, sautéed with
1 teaspoon butter, sprinkled with
1 teaspoon cinnamon sugar

(*Substitute:* Basic Breakfast 2)

**LUNCH**

Ham and Cheese Crunch
2 preformed taco shells
2 ounces (2 slices) lean ham, chopped
1 slice Lite-line cheese, shredded
Lettuce, shredded
Salsa to taste
1 cup skim milk

(*Substitute:* Basic Lunch 3)

**DINNER**

1 diet serving Turkey Curry
1 serving any Super Salad
1 cup skim milk

---

## *Broccoli-Rice Soup*

Prepare this soup ahead of time if you wish, but don't add the lemon juice, savory, or turkey until you're ready to serve it. Keep it covered in the refrigerator and reheat it slowly. Add the lemon juice and savory at the last minute and garnish with the turkey.

Don't freeze this soup.

2 packages frozen chopped broccoli
2 medium onions, minced
4 sprigs parsley, chopped
1 cup evaporated low-fat milk
2 cans condensed chicken broth, combined with 2 cans water
2 cups cooked brown rice
1 tablespoon whipped butter *or* diet margarine
½ tablespoon freshly squeezed lemon juice
1 teaspoon dried savory *or* 2 teaspoons chopped fresh
4 ounces smoked turkey breast, cut into thin strips.

Combine the broccoli, onions, parsley, milk, broth, and rice in a 3-quart saucepan. Bring to a boil, reduce the heat, and simmer about 20 minutes.

Remove from the heat and transfer half to a blender jar. Chop fine, but do not purée. Repeat with the remaining soup, returning both portions to the saucepan. Add the butter and stir until it melts and is fully incorporated.

Stir in the lemon juice and savory. Reheat quickly, and serve immediately, garnishing each portion with equal amounts of turkey.

*Yield: 6 diet servings*
*Calories per serving: 214*

## *BROCCOLI-RICE SOUP MENU PLAN*

*901 Calories (plus 200-calorie snack)*

Coffee, tea, or noncaloric beverages as desired

### BREAKFAST

1 small banana
½ cup plain low-fat yogurt
1 slice whole wheat toast

(*Substitute:* Basic Breakfast 2)

### LUNCH

English Cheeseburger
1 English muffin, toasted
2 ounces chopped lean meat, broiled, or
fried in nonstick pan
1 ounce Lite-line cheese
½ cup skim milk

(*Substitute:* Basic Lunch 1)

### DINNER

1 diet serving Broccoli-Rice Soup
1 serving any Super Salad
1 small tangerine
1 cup skim milk

## *Russian Stuffed Cabbage*

This dish may be served immediately, but its flavor improves considerably when it is allowed to stand, covered, in the refrigerator overnight.

Reheat it gently before serving.

1 medium savoy cabbage
8 ounces very lean ground round steak
1 small onion, finely chopped
½ cup brown rice
3 ounces plus 1 tablespoon canned tomato paste
¾ teaspoon cinnamon
1½ teaspoons salt
½ teaspoon freshly ground black pepper
1 tablespoon freshly squeezed lemon juice
1 tablespoon brown sugar

Remove the leaves from the cabbage and discard any that are damaged or bruised. Parboil them in water to cover until tender, taking care not to overcook them. Drain and cut off the hard stems and core from each leaf.

Combine the meat, onion, rice, 3 ounces tomato paste, cinnamon, salt, and pepper in a mixing bowl. Blend thoroughly. Set aside.

Choose 8 good-sized, undamaged leaves. Divide the meat mix among them, placing it in the lowest third (closest to you) of the leaf. Tuck in the sides and roll. Fix the overlapping seam with a wooden toothpick.

Line a 3-quart saucepan with the remaining cabbage, place the rolls on top of it, seam sides down, in one layer. Add just enough water to cover.

Combine the remaining tomato paste, the lemon juice, and sugar in a small bowl; mix and stir into the water in the saucepan.

Cover tightly and simmer gently 45 minutes. Add water

during cooking if necessary. Remove the cover and allow to cool in the cooking liquid.

Reheat gently and serve.

*Yield: 4 diet servings*
*Calories per serving: 315*

---

### RUSSIAN STUFFED CABBAGE MENU PLAN

*915 Calories (plus 200-calorie snack)*

Coffee, tea, or noncaloric beverages as desired

#### BREAKFAST

2 rice cakes
1 tablespoon diet jelly
1 cup skim milk

(*Substitute:* Basic Breakfast 1)

#### LUNCH

2 preformed taco shells
1 cup low-fat cottage cheese
1 cup fresh or unsweetened frozen strawberries

(*Substitute:* Basic Lunch 2)

#### DINNER

1 diet serving Russian Stuffed Cabbage
1 serving Super Spinach Salad

## Chinese Braised Beef

Are you chronically rushed at dinnertime? Make this dish early and let the meat soak up the lovely flavors of the sauce. Reheat it slowly while you prepare the rice for this complete one-dish dinner.

> 5 tablespoons soy sauce
> 2 tablespoons brown sugar
> 4 slices fresh ginger root *or* ½ teaspoon dried
> 1 whole star anise or 6 sections *or* ¼ teaspoon anise flavoring mixed with a pinch of cinnamon
> ½ cup cold water
> 2 tablespoons dry sherry
> 12 ounces very lean boneless beef shin
> ¾ cup white rice, cooked according to package directions

Combine the soy sauce, sugar, ginger, anise, water, and sherry in a mixing bowl. Stir until the sugar has completely dissolved and the ingredients are blended.

Put the beef in a heavy Dutch oven and pour the sauce over it. Bring to a boil, reduce the heat, cover tightly, and simmer very gently for approximately 2 hours. Turn the meat after the first hour, re-cover tightly, and continue cooking.

Check the pot periodically. If the liquid appears to be cooking out, make certain the heat is very low and add water, ¼ cup at a time, to keep the meat moist.

To serve, reheat the cooked rice and arrange it on a serving platter. Slice the meat very thin and arrange it over the rice. Pour the sauce over all.

*Yield: 4 diet servings*
*Calories per serving: 386*

### *CHINESE BRAISED BEEF MENU PLAN*

*897 Calories (plus 200-calorie snack)*

Coffee, tea, or noncaloric beverages as desired

## BREAKFAST

⅔ cup cooked Wheatena
1 teaspoon cinnamon sugar
1 cup skim milk

(*Substitute:* Basic Breakfast 3)

## LUNCH

Stuffed Tomato
   1 large tomato, scooped out
   2 ounces water-packed tuna
   1 green pepper, chopped
   1 tablespoon chopped parsley
   1 scallion, chopped (optional)
   1 tablespoon diet mayonnaise
1 1-ounce whole wheat bread pocket
1 cup skim milk

(*Substitute:* Basic Lunch 3)

## DINNER

1 diet serving Chinese Braised Beef

# Beef Persepolis

Darius, the unifier of the great ancient Persian empire, would have loved this dish. You will too. And you can prepare it long in advance and freeze it. To serve the frozen dish, thaw it in the refrigerator and reheat it quickly.

To freeze the rice, cook and season it, and toss it gently with a fork until it cools. Put it in a container and freeze it separately. To reheat, put a little water in a saucepan and add the frozen rice. Cook, covered, over moderate heat.

> 3 tablespoons whipped butter *or* diet margarine
> 2 medium onions, thinly sliced
> 12 ounces lean round steak, cut into ½-inch cubes
> ½ teaspoon salt
> ¼ teaspoon freshly ground black pepper
> 1 teaspoon cinnamon
> ¼ teaspoon nutmeg
> 1 beef bouillon cube, diluted in ½ cup boiling water
> ¾ cup chopped parsley
> ¼ cup chopped mint
> 3 cups diced celery, inner stalks only
> 2 tablespoons lemon juice
> 1 cup brown rice
> ½ teaspoon sugar

Melt 1 tablespoon butter in a large nonstick skillet and sauté the onion slices until they begin to brown. Transfer them to a small bowl and set aside.

Add the beef, salt, pepper, ½ teaspoon cinnamon, and nutmeg to the skillet and cook, stirring, over low heat until the meat browns slightly. Return the onions to the pan. Add the bouillon, cover tightly, and simmer 45 minutes or until the meat is tender. Add water, if necessary, to avoid burning. Try not to exceed ¼ cup.

Meanwhile, melt the remaining butter in a nonstick skillet. Add the parsley, mint, and celery. Sauté 10 minutes, stirring. Add the lemon juice, stir to mix, and pour over the beef.

Simmer 10 minutes longer. Cook the rice and toss with the remaining cinnamon and the sugar. Serve the meat over the rice.

*Yield: 6 diet servings*
*Calories per serving: 278*

---

### BEEF PERSEPOLIS MENU PLAN

*900 Calories (plus 200-calorie snack)*

Coffee, tea, or noncaloric beverages as desired

#### BREAKFAST

1 frozen waffle, topped with
½ cup low-fat cottage cheese and
½ banana, sliced

(*Substitute:* Basic Breakfast 1)

#### LUNCH

Turkey Pocket
2 ounces turkey
½ cucumber, chopped
1 scallion, chopped
Fresh or dried dill to taste
1 tablespoon diet mayonnaise
1 1-ounce whole wheat bread pocket
1 cup skim milk

(*Substitute:* Basic Lunch 3)

#### DINNER

1 diet serving Beef Persepolis
1 serving Super Spinach Salad
½ cup skim milk

## Spicy Pork with Cabbage

A quick, easy-to-prepare dish that's tasty and satisfying to eat. If you don't like your food spicy, omit the red pepper flakes and substitute freshly ground black pepper.

8 ounces lean pork, all visible fat removed, cut into matchstick slices
1 teaspoon salt
1 teaspoon sugar
1 tablespoon whiskey
4 tablespoons soy sauce
2 tablespoons sunflower *or* safflower oil
1½ pounds Chinese *or* savoy cabbage, tough core removed and finely shredded
1½ cloves garlic, finely minced
1 small piece (size of a quarter) fresh ginger, peeled and cut into matchstick slices
¼ teaspoon hot red pepper flakes
3 tablespoons chopped fresh coriander (optional)
¾ cup white rice, cooked according to package directions

Combine the pork, salt, sugar, whiskey, and half the soy sauce in a small bowl. Mix thoroughly and let stand 10 minutes.

Heat 1½ tablespoons oil in a well-seasoned wok or large nonstick skillet. Add the cabbage and sauté, stirring frequently, 5 minutes. Remove the cabbage with a slotted spoon and reserve.

Heat the remaining oil in the wok. Add the pork and its marinade, the garlic, and the ginger, and fry, stirring frequently, about 8 minutes or until all the meat is brown. Add the cabbage, pepper flakes, and remaining soy sauce. Reduce the heat to low, mix well, and cook, stirring occasionally, for an additional 8 minutes to reheat completely. Sprinkle with coriander.

Serve the meat and cabbage over the hot rice.

*Yield: 6 diet servings*
*Calories per serving: 277*

---

### *SPICY PORK WITH CABBAGE MENU PLAN*
*900 Calories (plus 200-calorie snack)*
Coffee, tea, or noncaloric beverages as desired

**BREAKFAST**

1 bran muffin
1 tablespoon diet jelly
1 cup skim milk

(*Substitute:* Basic Breakfast 1)

**LUNCH**

Grilled Tostada
2 frozen corn tortillas, heated in nonstick
pan
4 ounces lean cold cuts, heated in nonstick
pan
1 tomato
1 large dill pickle
Mustard to taste
1 cup skim milk

(*Substitute:* Basic Lunch 1)

**DINNER**

1 diet serving Spicy Pork with Cabbage
1 serving Super Spinach Salad
½ cup fresh or frozen unsweetened strawberries

## Yogurt Sour Soup

This soup may be served hot or chilled. To chill, let the soup cool to room temperature before putting it in the refrigerator.

Add a thin slice of lemon to the chopped cucumber and ham garnish when serving it cold.

> 1 cup plain low-fat yogurt
> 2 cups canned beef broth
> 4 ounces tofu, puréed
> 1 clove garlic, minced
> 2 cups cooked white rice
> Nonstick vegetable oil spray
> 2 teaspoons olive oil
> 2 tablespoons chopped parsley
> 2 medium onions, sliced very thin
> 1 tablespoon arrowroot *or* cornstarch, softened in 2
>     tablespoons water
> ½ teaspoon dill weed
> ½ cup coarsely chopped cucumber, sprinkled with
>     juice of ½ lemon
> 6 ounces cooked ham steak, cut into cubes

Combine the yogurt, broth, tofu, garlic, and 1½ cups rice in a blender. Liquefy. Transfer to a 1-quart saucepan. Cook over low heat 3 to 5 minutes, stirring occasionally. The yogurt must not boil.

Spray the bottom and sides of a 3-quart saucepan with nonstick vegetable oil; add the oil, parsley, and onions and toss. Cover the pan and cook, shaking it occasionally to keep from burning, until the onions are soft. Add 1 tablespoon of water if necessary to prevent them from browning. Add the arrowroot, then the remaining rice, and mix well.

Whisking continuously, slowly add the yogurt stock. Sprinkle in the dill and bring just to a boil. Reduce the heat and simmer until thick.

Remove from the heat, garnish with the cucumber and ham, and serve immediately.

*Yield: 6 diet servings*
*Calories per serving: 195*

---

### *YOGURT SOUR SOUP MENU PLAN*

*905 Calories (plus 200-calorie snack)*
Coffee, tea, or noncaloric beverages as desired

#### BREAKFAST

> 1 cup corn flakes
> 1 tablespoon raisins
> 1 cup skim milk

> (*Substitute:* Basic Breakfast 1)

#### LUNCH

Confetti Cottage Cheese
> 1 cup low-fat cottage cheese
> 1 carrot, chopped
> 1 tomato, chopped
> 1 tablespoon fresh dill *or* 1 teaspoon dried
> 1 tablespoon chopped parsley
> 1 teaspoon Worcestershire sauce (optional)
2 rice cakes

> (*Substitute:* Basic Lunch 2)

#### DINNER

> 1 diet serving Yogurt Sour Soup
> 1 serving Super Spinach Salad
> 1 ounce French bread
> ½ cup skim milk

## *Greek Fish Chowder*

Don't try to freeze this chowder. However, you may prepare it early in the day on which you plan to serve it. Reheat it gently to prevent the fish and potatoes from becoming mushy or dry.

> 1 pound cod, cusk, tilefish, or other firm, lean fish fillet
> ½ cup dry white wine
> ¼ cup water
> 8 chicken bouillon cubes, diluted in 5 cups boiling water
> 1 tablespoon freshly squeezed lemon juice
> 2 egg yolks, beaten with 2 tablespoons evaporated low-fat milk
> 1 cup cooked white rice, puréed
> 1 cup cooked brown rice
> 1 pound potatoes, peeled, cooked, and kept warm
> Pinch of thyme
> Salt and freshly ground black pepper to taste

Combine the fish, wine, and water in a skillet. Cover and poach until the fish is cooked through and flakes easily with a fork. Drain and reserve the poaching liquid and fish separately.

Place the bouillon, lemon juice, and liquid in which the fish was poached in a 3-quart saucepan or stockpot. Bring the stock just to the boiling point and remove from the heat.

Slowly, stirring constantly, add 1 cup of the hot stock to the egg yolks. Pour the heated yolks into the remaining stock, stirring continually.

Stir in the white rice, brown rice, and potatoes. Set the heat low and return the stock to it. Keep stirring to incorporate the egg completely as it cooks.

When the soup has thickened somewhat, add the fish

flakes, sprinkle with thyme, and season with salt and pepper. Garnish with lemon slices if desired.

*Yield: 6 diet servings*
*Calories per serving: 217*

---

## *GREEK FISH CHOWDER MENU PLAN*

*911 Calories (plus 200-calorie snack)*

Coffee, tea, or noncaloric beverages as desired

### BREAKFAST

1 egg, any style (use nonstick pan to scramble or fry)
1 slice Canadian bacon, broiled
½ slice rye toast

(*Substitute:* Basic Breakfast 4)

### LUNCH

2 rice cakes, topped with
2 ounces skim-milk mozzarella cheese
1 cup skim milk

(*Substitute:* Basic Lunch 3)

### DINNER

1 diet serving Greek Fish Chowder
1 serving Super Spinach Salad
½ cup diced canned pineapple in juice
1 cup skim milk

## *Halibut à la Russe*

A good choice for a family of four with one dieter. For two people, with one on the diet, divide the recipe in half.

Nonstick vegetable oil spray
5 tablespoons flour
¼ teaspoon freshly ground black pepper
½ teaspoon coarse salt
6 halibut steaks (1½ pounds maximum total weight)
2 tablespoons whipped butter *or* diet margarine
1 medium onion, finely chopped
1 clove garlic, minced
2 tablespoons sliced almonds
1 medium can whole tomatoes, drained
1 tablespoon tomato paste
½ cup canned condensed chicken broth, diluted
   with ½ cup water
1 teaspoon freshly squeezed lemon juice
4 tablespoons Sour Half-and-Half (page 28)
2 cups cooked white rice, kept warm

Prepare a casserole or baking dish, large enough to hold the fish in one layer, by spraying the bottom and sides with non-stick vegetable oil. Set aside.

Combine 3 tablespoons flour, the pepper, and the salt in a small bowl, and mix well. Place the fish on a platter and sprinkle with half the seasoned flour.

Spray a nonstick skillet, large enough to hold all the fish steaks, with nonstick vegetable oil. Melt 1 tablespoon butter, add the fish, and brown quickly on the floured side. Sprinkle the top with the remaining seasoned flour, turn, and brown. Transfer the fish to the prepared casserole and set aside.

Melt the remaining butter in the skillet. Combine the onions, garlic, and almonds and add to the skillet. Cook gently until the onions are soft and the almonds begin to brown. Stir in the remaining unseasoned flour and cook a few minutes. Do not allow to brown. Stir in the tomatoes, tomato paste, broth, and lemon juice. Bring to a boil, stirring. Cook until the sauce begins to thicken. Remove from the heat. Stir in the half-and-half and pour the sauce over the fish. Cover and bake in a preheated 325°F oven 30 minutes or until the fish flakes with a fork. Serve over rice.

*Yield: 6 diet servings*
*Calories per serving: 282*

---

## HALIBUT À LA RUSSE MENU PLAN
*892 Calories (plus 200-calorie snack)*
Coffee, tea, or noncaloric beverages as desired

**BREAKFAST**    (*Substitute:* Basic Breakfast 2)

½ cup fresh or unsweetened frozen strawberries
1 slice cooked lean ham
1 slice frozen French toast
½ cup skim milk

**LUNCH**    (*Substitute:* Basic Lunch 2)

Green and White Tomato
    1 large tomato, stuffed with
    5 ounces tofu
    1 tablespoon chopped parsley
    1 scallion, chopped
    1 tablespoon diet salad dressing
1 1-ounce whole wheat bread pocket, toasted

**DINNER**

1 diet serving Halibut à la Russe
1 cup cooked carrots
½ serving Super Spinach Salad
½ cup skim milk

## *Cod in Caper Sauce*

This is a tasty and nutritious way to prepare cod or any other low-fat, firm-fleshed white fish. The nutty flavor of the brown rice is an excellent complement to the tart flavor of the caper sauce. A leftover serving may be enjoyed cold the next day.

> Nonstick vegetable oil spray
> 2 tablespoons whipped butter *or* diet margarine
> 1 tablespoon flour
> ⅔ cup dry white wine
> 2 onions, finely minced
> 1 small clove garlic, finely minced
> 2 tablespoons tomato paste
> ½ tablespoon chopped capers
> 4 teaspoons white wine vinegar
> Generous pinch salt and pepper
> 1½ pounds fresh cod fillet
> 1 cup brown rice, cooked according to package directions
> 1 teaspoon chopped fresh dill *or* ¼ teaspoon dried
> Parsley for garnish (optional)

Prepare a small baking dish, one that will just hold the fish, by spraying with nonstick vegetable oil. Set aside.

Melt 1 tablespoon butter in a small saucepan, add the flour, and blend. Add the wine, stirring constantly. Cook, stirring, until smooth. Remove from the heat and reserve.

Melt the remaining butter in a small nonstick skillet. Add the onions and garlic and sauté until soft. Add the tomato paste, capers, 3 teaspoons vinegar, salt, and pepper. Cook, over low heat, 5 minutes. Add the vegetable mixture to the wine in the saucepan and simmer an additional 5 minutes. Turn the sauce into a blender or food processor fitted with a metal blade and purée.

Wipe the fish fillet with the remaining vinegar and arrange in the baking dish. Pour the sauce over the fish and bake in a preheated 350°F oven 20 minutes until the fish flakes easily.

Meanwhile, prepare the rice, sprinkle it with the dill, and toss. Arrange a bed of rice on a platter; place the baked fish on the rice and spoon the sauce over both.

*Yield: 6 diet servings*
*Calories per serving: 240*

---

### COD IN CAPER SAUCE MENU PLAN

*903 Calories (plus 200-calorie snack)*
Coffee, tea, or noncaloric beverages as desired

**BREAKFAST**

½ banana, sliced, mixed with
½ cup low-fat cottage cheese and
¼ cup plain low-fat yogurt
2 Melba toast rounds

(*Substitute:* Basic Breakfast 4)

**LUNCH**

Wry Cheese
  2 ounces Lite-line cheese
  2 slices rye toast
  Mustard *or* 1 tablespoon diet margarine *or*
    diet mayonnaise
½ cup skim milk

(*Substitute:* Basic Lunch 2)

**DINNER**

1 diet serving Cod in Caper Sauce
⅔ cup cooked broccoli
1 serving Basic Super Salad
1 cup fresh or unsweetened frozen strawberries

## *Rumanian Salmon*

It's unlikely you've come across this dish before, but if you like garlic, this Rumanian favorite is its own reward.

This dish *must* be made at least one hour before serving, but may be made even earlier and refrigerated, then brought back to room temperature before serving. However, be forewarned: if this dish is not tightly covered while it's in the refrigerator it will impart its garlic flavor to everything else.

> 1 cup water
> 1 teaspoon cider vinegar
> 1 slice lemon
> 2 peppercorns, whole
> 2 sprigs parsley
> ¼ teaspoon salt
> 1 whole clove
> 1 small bay leaf
> 1 pound salmon, cut into 6 steaks
> 4 cloves garlic
> Juice of 1 lemon, freshly squeezed
> ¼ teaspoon salt
> ⅛ teaspoon hot pepper flakes
> 2 tablespoons finely chopped parsley
> Lemon slices
> 3 cups cooked brown rice

Combine the water, vinegar, lemon slice, peppercorns, parsley, salt, clove, and bay leaf in a skillet that will hold the steaks in one layer. Bring to a boil, reduce the heat, and simmer 5 minutes. Add the salmon steaks and poach, covered, 3 minutes or until the salmon is opaque but still firm. Remove the pan from the heat, keeping it covered.

Place the garlic in a mortar and crush it with a pestle. Add the lemon juice and salt and continue to crush the garlic until it is liquefied and the salt has dissolved. Stir in the pepper flakes.

Brush each salmon steak with the sauce until it has all been used. Cover and let stand 1 hour.

Garnish with parsley and lemon slices and serve at room temperature, accompanied by the rice.

*Yield: 6 diet servings*
*Calories per serving: 254*

---

### RUMANIAN SALMON MENU PLAN

*896 Calories (plus 200-calorie snack)*

Coffee, tea, or noncaloric beverages as desired

#### BREAKFAST

1 corn muffin
½ cup plain low-fat yogurt

(*Substitute:* Basic Breakfast 4)

#### LUNCH

Cucumber Boats
    1 large cucumber, seeds removed, filled with
    1 cup low-fat cottage cheese, mixed with
    1 tablespoon dry onion soup mix
    1 scallion (optional)
½ green pepper, cut in strips
1 English muffin, toasted

(*Substitute:* Basic Lunch 2)

#### DINNER

1 diet serving Rumanian Salmon
1 cup cooked carrots
½ serving Super Spinach Salad
½ cup skim milk

## *Italian Shrimp Soup*

You may prepare this soup as early as the day before you are going to serve it, but don't add the shrimp until the soup has been reheated. Then continue with the recipe.

> Nonstick vegetable oil spray
> 1 tablespoon whipped butter *or* diet margarine
> 1 small onion, chopped
> 1 small carrot, chopped
> ¼ teaspoon dried thyme *or* ½ teaspoon fresh
> 1 bay leaf
> 2 teaspoons chopped fresh parsley
> ¼ cup reserved shrimp liquid
> 4 ounces dry red wine
> 5 cubes chicken bouillon, dissolved in 5 cups boiling
> water
> 1½ cups white rice
> 1 can wet-pack tiny shrimp, drained, liquid reserved
> 2 drops Tabasco sauce
> Salt and pepper to taste
> 1 tablespoon Sour Half-and-Half (page 28)

Spray a 3-quart nonstick saucepan with nonstick vegetable oil. Add the butter, onion, carrot, and herbs.

Stirring, brown the onions gently over moderate heat, add the shrimp liquid, and cook, stirring, 10 minutes. (Measure the reserved shrimp liquid and, if necessary, add water to make ¼ cup. If there is more, add the excess liquid to the bouillon.)

Add the wine, cover, and simmer 15 minutes.

Combine the bouillon and rice in a second saucepan. Bring to a boil, cover, and cook 20 minutes or until the rice is soft. Strain the rice, reserving the bouillon. Add the rice to the vegetables in the first saucepan.

Discard the bay leaf and purée the rice and vegetables

with their cooking liquid. Add the shrimp to the purée and combine with the reserved bouillon. Bring all back to a boil. Remove from the heat, add the Tabasco sauce and correct seasoning. Stir in half-and-half.

*Yield: 6 diet servings*
*Calories per serving: 238*

---

### ITALIAN SHRIMP SOUP MENU PLAN

*908 Calories (plus 200-calorie snack)*

Coffee, tea, or noncaloric beverages as desired

**BREAKFAST**

1 slice cooked lean ham
1 slice Swiss cheese, melted, on
1 slice rye toast

(*Substitute:* Basic Breakfast 4)

**LUNCH**

1 cup low-fat cottage cheese, mixed with
1 teaspoon cinnamon sugar and
1 banana, chopped
1 1-ounce whole wheat bread pocket, toasted

(*Substitute:* Basic Lunch 2)

**DINNER**

1 diet serving Italian Shrimp Soup
1 serving Basic Super Salad
1 cup skim milk

# Baked Shrimpies 'n' Rice

If you're looking for an easy recipe, this is it. Save it for one of those days when the dog has chewed your favorite slippers, your car died in the busiest intersection in town, and you've finally gotten home only to realize you forgot to turn off Mr. Coffee that morning.

It's quick, it's easy, and it satisfies.

2 cups cooked rice, cooled
1 cup crab meat, picked over and flaked
1 cup cooked shrimp, sliced in half
1 small green pepper, chopped
3 scallions, white parts only, trimmed and finely chopped
1 cup celery, finely chopped
1 package frozen peas, cooked and cooled
½ teaspoon salt
½ teaspoon freshly ground black pepper
½ teaspoon Worcestershire sauce
Nonstick vegetable oil spray
2 tablespoons grated Parmesan cheese

Combine the rice, crab meat, shrimp, green pepper, scallions, celery, peas, salt, pepper, and Worcestershire in a large mixing bowl and toss to mix well.

Prepare an attractive, ovenproof casserole by spraying it lightly with nonstick vegetable oil. Turn the seafood mix into it; sprinkle with cheese and bake 30 minutes in a preheated 325°F oven.

Serve directly from the casserole.

*Yield: 4 diet servings*
*Calories per serving: 279*

# *BAKED SHRIMPIES 'N' RICE MENU PLAN*

*906 Calories (plus 200-calorie snack)*

Coffee, tea, or noncaloric beverages as desired

## BREAKFAST

½ bagel, toasted
1 teaspoon peanut butter
1 teaspoon diet jelly
1 cup skim milk

(*Substitute:* Basic Breakfast 1)

## LUNCH

Ham on Rye
    2 slices lean canned ham (2 ounces)
    2 slices rye bread
    Mustard
1 dill pickle
½ cup skim milk

(*Substitute:* Basic Lunch 1)

## DINNER

1 diet serving Baked Shrimpies 'n' Rice
1 serving Super Coleslaw
½ cup fresh or unsweetened frozen strawberries

❧ *Eat by candlelight. It takes longer
because it's harder to see the food.*

## *Risotto Marinara*

When we think of Italy we usually think of pasta and pizza, but in northern Italy rice and cornmeal are the dishes of preference. A risotto, golden with saffron, is recognized by any Milanese as a native dish.

Cold leftovers are good the next day.

> Nonstick vegetable oil spray
> 1 tablespoon olive oil
> 1 medium onion, finely chopped
> 2 cloves garlic, finely chopped
> 4 inner stalks celery, sliced
> ½ cup canned chopped pimientos, drained
> 2 cups canned condensed chicken broth, diluted
>     with ¼ cup water
> 1 cup white rice
> 1 can (7½ ounces) crab meat, well picked over and
>     flaked
> 8 ounces fresh or frozen raw shrimp, shelled and de-
>     veined
> 2 tablespoons tomato paste
> 1 teaspoon salt
> ¼ teaspoon pepper
> Pinch cayenne pepper
> 3 strands Spanish saffron
> 1 ounce Parmesan cheese, grated

Prepare a casserole or baking dish by spraying with nonstick vegetable oil.

Heat the olive oil in a large nonstick skillet for which you have a cover. Add the onion and garlic; sauté until soft but not brown. Add the celery and pimientos and continue to cook until the celery is soft. Add the broth and bring to a boil.

Combine the rice, crab, and shrimp and add them to the skillet. Stir in the tomato paste, salt, pepper, cayenne, and saffron until the paste has dissolved. Bring the broth to a boil again, taste, and correct seasoning.

Turn everything into the prepared casserole and bake 30 minutes in a preheated 350°F oven. Sprinkle with grated cheese.

*Yield: 6 diet servings*
*Calories per serving: 262*

---

### *RISOTTO MARINARA MENU PLAN*

*896 Calories (plus 200-calorie snack)*
Coffee, tea, or noncaloric beverages as desired

### BREAKFAST

    1 small orange
    ½ English muffin, toasted
    1 teaspoon diet jelly
    1 cup skim milk

    (*Substitute:* Basic Breakfast 4)

### LUNCH

    Ham and Cheese Taco
      2 preformed taco shells
      2 ounces (2 slices) lean ham, chopped
      1 slice Lite-line cheese, shredded
      Lettuce, shredded
      Salsa to taste
    1 cup skim milk

    (*Substitute:* Basic Lunch 3)

### DINNER

    1 diet serving Risotto Marinara
    1 serving any Super Salad
    1 cup fresh or unsweetened frozen strawberries

## *Quick Foo Yong*

Everybody loves foo yong, so you may want to make more than two servings. This recipe can very easily be multiplied; simply double, triple, or quadruple the called-for amounts. However, unless you're an expert pancake flipper, you will have to fry each two-serving foo yong separately.

> 1 tablespoon vegetable oil
> 2 scallions, thinly sliced on the diagonal
> 6 medium-sized fresh mushrooms, scrubbed, trimmed, and thinly sliced
> 3 eggs, lightly beaten
> 2 teaspoons sugar
> ¼ teaspoon salt
> 2 teaspoons dry sherry
> ½ cup canned crab meat, picked over and flaked
> ¼ cup fresh or frozen (thawed) green peas
> ½ cup cooked brown rice
> ½ cup chicken broth
> 1 teaspoon cornstarch, softened in 2 teaspoons water
> 1 tablespoon chopped fresh coriander *or* parsley

Heat 1 teaspoon oil in a medium-sized nonstick skillet. Add the scallions and mushrooms and sauté quickly until just barely soft. Remove and set aside.

Combine the eggs, 1 teaspoon sugar, salt, sherry, crab meat, peas, and rice and stir lightly to mix.

Combine the broth, cornstarch, remaining teaspoon sugar, and coriander in a separate small bowl. Set aside.

Add the remaining oil to the skillet and heat. Add the egg mixture all at once and stir gently with a wooden spoon or spatula until the eggs begin to set. Spread them out to the edges of the pan and cook over high heat until the bottom is lightly browned. Turn and brown other side. Remove to a heated platter.

Turn the sauce into the skillet and cook, stirring, until it thickens slightly. Pour over the eggs and serve.

*Yield: 2 diet servings*
*Calories per serving: 313*

---

## QUICK FOO YONG MENU PLAN

*894 Calories (plus 200-calorie snack)*

Coffee, tea, or noncaloric beverages as desired

### BREAKFAST

½ cup orange juice *or* ½ sliced banana
1 cup bran flakes *or* Cheerios
1 cup skim milk

(*Substitute:* Basic Breakfast 1)

### LUNCH

3 ounces lean chopped beef, broiled, or fried in
    nonstick pan
½ serving Super Coleslaw
2 rice cakes
½ cup skim milk

(*Substitute:* Basic Lunch 1)

### DINNER

1 diet serving Quick Foo Yong
½ serving Super Coleslaw
½ cup skim milk

## New Orleans Crab

By all means, serve our New Orleans Crab immediately, as
the recipe requires, but leftovers may be served cold *the next
day;* toss them with 1 teaspoon Raspberry Vinegar (page 24)
for each leftover serving.

>     1 package frozen artichokes, cooked with
>     4 slices lemon
>     2 tablespoons whipped butter *or* diet margarine
>     ½ pound mushrooms, sliced
>     1 tablespoon plus 2 teaspoons freshly squeezed
>         lemon juice
>     10 small scallions, white and green parts, trimmed
>         and finely chopped
>     1 clove garlic, minced
>     4 tablespoons minced parsley
>     1 pound crab meat, carefully picked over and flaked
>     Salt and white pepper to taste
>     1 cup cooked brown rice

Drain the artichokes and discard the lemon. Cut each artichoke into quarters and set aside.

Melt 1 tablespoon butter in a large nonstick skillet; add the
mushrooms, sprinkle with 2 teaspoons lemon juice, and sauté
gently, until most of the liquid has evaporated.

Add the remaining butter, half the scallions, the garlic, and
half the parsley. Sauté, stirring gently, until soft. Stir in the
artichoke quarters.

Using a plastic spatula or spoon, fold in the crab meat, the
remaining lemon juice, and salt and pepper to taste. Cook 3
to 5 minutes or until heated through. Add the remaining
scallions and parsley, toss, and serve immediately, accompanied by the rice.

*Yield: 4 diet servings*
*Calories per serving: 234*

## NEW ORLEANS CRAB MENU PLAN

*899 Calories (plus 200-calorie snack)*

Coffee, tea, or noncaloric beverages as desired

### BREAKFAST

⅓ medium cantaloupe
1-egg omelet, cooked in nonstick pan with
½ slice Lite-line cheese
1 slice whole wheat toast

(*Substitute:* Basic Breakfast 2)

### LUNCH

Muenster Pocket
    2 ounces Muenster cheese
    1 green pepper, chopped
    Alfalfa sprouts to taste
    1 1-ounce whole wheat bread pocket

(*Substitute:* Basic Lunch 2)

### DINNER

1 diet serving New Orleans Crab
½ serving Basic Super Salad
1 cup cooked carrots
1 cup skim milk

❧ *A glass of wine has 100 calories.*
*Would you rather have two glasses*
*of wine or your carbohydrate snack?*

## Stir-Fry Scallop Crunch

This quick, easy, and delightfully tasty adaptation of a traditional Chinese dish takes no longer to prepare than the time
required to boil the rice.

> ¾ cup white rice
> ¾ pound fresh sea scallops
> 2 tablespoons sunflower or safflower oil
> 2 medium onions, finely chopped
> 1 sweet red *or* green pepper, washed, seeded, and
>     cut into ½-inch squares
> 12 canned water chestnuts, coarsely chopped
> 1 teaspoon salt
> ¼ teaspoon black pepper
> 4 eggs, lightly beaten
> 1 tablespoon soy sauce
> 5 scallions, white and green parts, trimmed and
>     thinly sliced

Cook the rice according to package directions. Meanwhile,
cut the scallops into quarters. Reserve.

Heat the oil in a well-seasoned wok or nonstick skillet. Add
the onions, red or green pepper, water chestnuts, salt, and
pepper. Fry, stirring frequently, about 5 minutes. Add the
scallops and cook an additional 5 minutes. Stir to prevent the
onions and scallops from burning. Reduce the heat.

Combine the eggs, soy sauce, and scallions. Mix well.

Pour the eggs over the scallops and cook gently until the
eggs have set to your taste.

Serve over the rice.

> *Yield: 6 diet servings*
> *Calories per serving: 264*

## *STIR-FRY SCALLOP CRUNCH MENU PLAN*

*901 Calories (plus 200-calorie snack)*

Coffee, tea, or noncaloric beverages as desired

### BREAKFAST

1 frozen waffle
½ cup plain low-fat yogurt
½ cup fresh or unsweetened frozen blueberries
1 teaspoon sugar

(*Substitute:* Basic Breakfast 3)

### LUNCH

Pepper Steak Pocket
    4 ounces lean beef cold cuts, warmed in non-stick pan
    1 green pepper and
    1 small onion, chopped and sautéed in
    1 teaspoon oil, sprinkled with
    Oregano and basil
    1 1-ounce whole wheat bread pocket

(*Substitute:* Basic Lunch 1)

### DINNER

1 diet serving Stir-Fry Scallop Crunch
½ serving any Super Salad
5 large whole strawberries
1 cup skim milk

# 7

---

# *Grains*

### *Chicken Yucatán*

You may prepare this casserole and arrange the ingredients early in the day. Follow the recipe for preparation, but don't bake it. Store it in the refrigerator.

At dinnertime bake the dish in a preheated 375°F oven according to the directions.

> Nonstick vegetable oil spray
> 1 tablespoon olive oil
> 1 onion, finely chopped
> 1 clove garlic, finely chopped
> 1 teaspoon salt
> ⅓ cup tomato paste
> 2 cups canned tomatoes
> 10 ripe pitted black olives, sliced
> ¾ cup cornmeal
> 2 teaspoons chili powder
> 3 cups canned chicken broth
> 2 cups cooked frozen (thawed) or leftover chicken, cubed

Prepare a casserole or baking dish by spraying the bottom and sides with nonstick vegetable oil. Set aside.

Heat the oil in a large nonstick skillet. Add the onion and garlic and cook until soft. Stir in the salt, tomato paste, tomatoes, olives, cornmeal, chili, and broth. Mix well.

Cook over low heat until thick — about 15 minutes. Add the chicken, stir, and turn into the prepared casserole.

Bake, uncovered, in a preheated 375 °F oven 30 to 40 minutes or until brown. The dish should be quite moist. If it appears to be too thick, add water to thin.

*Yield: 6 diet servings*
*Calories per serving: 240*

---

### CHICKEN YUCATÁN MENU PLAN

*849 Calories (plus 200-calorie snack)*
Coffee, tea, or noncaloric beverages as desired

**BREAKFAST**

1 egg, boiled, or cooked in nonstick pan
1 sausage link
1 slice whole wheat toast
½ cup skim milk

(*Substitute:* Basic Breakfast 4)

**LUNCH**

Wry Cheese Sandwich
  1 ounce Swiss cheese
  2 slices rye bread
  Mustard
1 green pepper *or* 1 carrot
½ cup skim milk

(*Substitute:* Basic Lunch 4)

**DINNER**

1 diet serving Chicken Yucatán
½ serving Super Coleslaw
1 cup skim milk

## Chicken Livers Milanese

East meets West in this dish. These Chinese-style chicken livers served over Italian-style cornmeal afford a unique combination of flavors.

You may marinate the livers early in the day and finish the dish at dinnertime.

> 4 tablespoons soy sauce
> 2 tablespoons honey
> ½ clove garlic, finely minced
> Pinch salt
> 9 ounces chicken livers, membranes removed, cut into quarters
> 1 small can water chestnuts, drained and quartered
> ½ cup dry white wine
> 1 tablespoon cornstarch, softened in 2 tablespoons water
> 4 cups cooked cornmeal, kept warm

Combine the soy sauce, honey, garlic, and salt in a medium-sized bowl. Stir until the honey dissolves. Add the livers and water chestnuts and marinate at least 2 hours, turning occasionally.

Turn the marinade, livers, and chestnuts into a small saucepan, add the wine, and simmer gently until the livers are cooked through. (Test by cutting into a liver.)

Remove the livers and chestnuts to a warm plate with a slotted spoon.

Add the cornstarch to the marinade in the saucepan. Bring to a boil and cook, stirring, until it thickens to the consistency of heavy cream. Return the livers and chestnuts to the sauce to reheat.

Place the cornmeal on a serving platter and press into the center with a large spoon to produce a well. Turn the meat and sauce into the well and serve.

*Yield: 6 diet servings*
*Calories per serving: 228*

## *CHICKEN LIVERS MILANESE MENU PLAN*

*904 Calories (plus 200-calorie snack)*

Coffee, tea, or noncaloric beverages as desired

### BREAKFAST

½ cup fresh or unsweetened frozen blueberries
½ cup vanilla-flavored low-fat yogurt
½ English muffin, toasted

(*Substitute:* Basic Breakfast 3)

### LUNCH

Tuna Melt
2 slices whole wheat bread
2 ounces water-packed tuna
1 ounce skim-milk mozzarella cheese
Melt under broiler.
½ cup skim milk

(*Substitute:* Basic Lunch 1)

### DINNER

1 diet serving Chicken Livers Milanese
3 stalks broccoli
1 cup skim milk

୬ *Eating to procrastinate never works.*
*You end up feeling guilty about two*
*things: the unfinished task and the*
*excess calories.*

## *Rumanian Stew*

To prepare this stew the day before, use a dish that can go right from the refrigerator into a hot oven. To reheat, add ¼ cup vegetable juice cocktail and bake in a preheated 375°F oven, covered, for 10 to 15 minutes.

Nonstick vegetable oil spray
2 cups water
1½ teaspoons salt
1 cup cornmeal
8 ounces lean pork loin, cut into 6 thin cutlets
2 tablespoons whipped butter *or* diet margarine
4 ripe tomatoes, thickly sliced
2 medium onions, thinly sliced
1 sweet red pepper, seeded and thinly sliced
½ pound mushrooms, scrubbed, trimmed, and sliced
2 cups diced eggplant
1 package frozen string beans, thawed and drained
1 chicken bouillon cube, in ½ cup boiling water
1 cup vegetable juice cocktail, seasoned with
Generous dashes Tabasco and Worcestershire sauces

Prepare a deep covered casserole by spraying the bottom and sides with nonstick vegetable oil. Set aside.

Bring water and 1 teaspoon salt to a boil in a large saucepan. Stirring, slowly pour in the cornmeal. Reduce the heat and stir until the cornmeal is thick. Cook 10 more minutes and turn into the casserole. Smooth and set aside.

Place the cutlets between two sheets of wax paper and pound until very thin.

Melt 1 tablespoon butter and brush it over the bottom of a large nonstick skillet. Brown the cutlets quickly on both sides. Transfer them to the casserole. Top with the tomatoes and sprinkle with ¼ teaspoon salt. Add the remaining butter, onions, peppers, and mushrooms and sauté until soft. Add eggplant and sauté until soft and brown. Remove from the heat, add the string beans, and toss to mix. Turn the vegetables into the casserole; sprinkle with the remaining salt.

Add the bouillon and seasoned vegetable juice to the skillet and deglaze over high heat.

Pour the liquid into the casserole, cover, and bake in a preheated 375°F oven about 1 hour or until the meat is tender and most of the liquid has been absorbed.

*Yield: 6 diet servings*
*Calories per serving: 258*

---

### *RUMANIAN STEW MENU PLAN*
*885 Calories (plus 200-calorie snack)*
Coffee, tea, or noncaloric beverages as desired

**BREAKFAST**    (*Substitute:* Basic Breakfast 2)

1 cup tomato juice
1 poached egg
1 slice whole wheat toast
1 teaspoon diet margarine

**LUNCH**    (*Substitute:* Basic Lunch 3)

Tostada with Cheese
  2 frozen corn tortillas, heated
  2 ounces shredded Lite-line cheese
  ½ green pepper, chopped
  ½ medium tomato, chopped
  Chopped chili peppers *or* salsa to taste
1 cup skim milk

**DINNER**

1 diet serving Rumanian Stew
1 cup skim milk
1 cup fresh or unsweetened frozen strawberries

# Southern Corn Casserole

This simple-to-prepare and delicious entrée will remain a favorite long after you've reached your ideal weight.

While this dish is more like a pudding than a soufflé, it should be eaten soon after preparation for maximum flavor.

> 2 packages frozen corn kernels, cooked, drained,
> and slightly cooled
> 1 tablespoon whipped butter *or* diet margarine,
> melted
> ¾ cup low-fat milk
> ½ pound raw shrimp, peeled and deveined
> ½ pound raw scallops, cut into quarters
> 3 eggs, separated
> ½ teaspoon salt (less if desired)
> ¼ teaspoon white pepper
> Nonstick vegetable oil spray

Combine the corn, butter, milk, shrimp, scallops, egg yolks, salt, and pepper. Mix gently, but thoroughly.

Beat the egg whites until stiff but not dry. Fold them into the corn mixture.

Spray the bottom and sides of a medium-sized ovenproof casserole or baking dish with nonstick vegetable oil and turn the corn mixture into it.

Bake in a preheated 300°F oven 30 minutes or until a cake tester or sharp knife comes out clean.

> *Yield: 4 diet servings*
> *Calories per serving: 240*

## SOUTHERN CORN CASSEROLE MENU PLAN

*888 Calories (plus 200-calorie snack)*

Coffee, tea, or noncaloric beverages as desired

### BREAKFAST

1 cup plain low-fat yogurt
½ cup fresh or unsweetened frozen blueberries
1 rice cake

(*Substitute:* Basic Breakfast 1)

### LUNCH

Crunchy Egg Salad
   1 hard-boiled egg, chopped
   1 small tomato, chopped
   ½ cucumber, chopped
   1 scallion, chopped (optional)
1 1-ounce whole wheat bread pocket
1 cup skim milk

(*Substitute:* Basic Lunch 3)

### DINNER

1 diet serving Southern Corn Casserole
½ serving any Super Salad

*If you succumb to temptation and
eat something highly caloric, skip
the next meal. The calories will
equal out.*

## Sweet Cheese Pudding

Prepare this pudding early in the day and serve it at room temperature, or bake it just before serving and cool it slightly.

> 1½ cups kasha
> 2 cups water
> 2 cups low-fat cottage cheese
> 1 teaspoon vegetable oil
> 2 tablespoons bread crumbs, unseasoned
> 2 tablespoons whipped butter *or* diet margarine, melted
> 3 eggs
> 4 tablespoons confectioners sugar
> ¼ cup Sour Half-and-Half (page 28)
> ⅔ cup plain low-fat yogurt
> ½ teaspoon vanilla
> Pinch salt

Cook the kasha in the water, following the directions on the package but omitting the egg and butter.

While the kasha is cooking, cream the cheese in a blender or food processor and rub the oil on the bottom and sides of a medium-sized baking dish. Pat the sides and bottom with the bread crumbs so they adhere to the oil. Set aside.

When the kasha is cooked, stir in the butter and blend. Add the cheese, mix thoroughly, and turn into the casserole.

Combine the eggs, sugar, half-and-half, yogurt, vanilla, and salt in a small bowl. Whisk until thoroughly blended and pour over the kasha.

Bake, uncovered, 30 minutes in a preheated 350°F oven. Allow to cool slightly and serve.

*Yield: 6 diet servings*
*Calories per serving: 309*

## SWEET CHEESE PUDDING MENU PLAN

*904 Calories (plus 200-calorie snack)*

Coffee, tea, or noncaloric beverages as desired

### BREAKFAST

1 poached egg
1 slice cooked lean ham
1 slice whole wheat toast

(*Substitute:* Basic Breakfast 4)

### LUNCH

3 ounces lean chopped beef, broiled, or fried in
    nonstick pan
½ serving Super Coleslaw
2 rice cakes
½ cup skim milk

(*Substitute:* Basic Lunch 1)

### DINNER

1 diet serving Sweet Cheese Pudding
1 cup fresh or unsweetened frozen strawberries

⋐ *Crunchy, undercooked vegetables
take more time to eat than mushy
ones. Steam or blanch them quickly
in boiling water to increase your
chewing time.*

## *Rumanian Chicken Salad*

This salad should be prepared ahead of time.

    ¼ cup white wine
    ½ cup water
    12 ounces chicken breast, boned, skinned, and all
        visible fat removed
    ½ cup kasha
    1 egg
    1 cup boiling water
    2 ounces dried French *or* Italian bread
    3 tablespoons tarragon vinegar, mixed with ¼ cup
        water
    3 hard-boiled eggs, yolks and whites chopped sepa-
        rately
    1 tablespoon chopped capers
    1 teaspoon ground sage
    1 tablespoon olive oil
    2 tablespoons wine vinegar
    4 tablespoons chopped chives
    1 tablespoon chopped parsley

Combine the wine, ½ cup water, and chicken in a small skillet. Poach gently until the chicken is cooked. Drain, chill,
and cut into thin strips.

Cook the kasha according to the directions on the package,
using the egg and boiling water. Cool and set aside.

Soak the bread in the tarragon vinegar mixture. Squeeze
dry and chop fine. Add the egg yolk. Sprinkle with the
capers, sage, oil, and vinegar. Mix thoroughly and set aside.

To assemble, add 3 tablespoons chives to the cooled kasha
and toss to mix. Turn onto a decorative serving platter and
gently press out toward the edges to produce a layer of kasha.

Press the seasoned bread/egg mixture through a coarse
sieve onto the kasha.

Arrange the chicken slices over the bread mixture and

sprinkle with parsley, the remaining chives, and egg white. Chill at least 2 hours.

*Yield: 6 diet servings*
*Calories per serving: 281*

---

### RUMANIAN CHICKEN SALAD MENU PLAN

*900 Calories (plus 200-calorie snack)*
Coffee, tea, or noncaloric beverages as desired

**BREAKFAST**

1 bran muffin
1 teaspoon diet jelly
1 cup skim milk

(*Substitute:* Basic Breakfast 1)

**LUNCH**

Grilled Tostada
2 frozen corn tortillas, heated in nonstick
    pan
4 ounces lean cold cuts, heated in nonstick
    pan
1 tomato
1 large dill pickle
Mustard to taste
1 cup skim milk

(*Substitute:* Basic Lunch 1)

**DINNER**

1 diet serving Rumanian Chicken Salad
1 serving Basic Super Salad
½ cup fresh or unsweetened frozen strawberries

---

## Stuffed Beefsteak

You'll find this an easy and very satisfying dish to prepare. Be sure to remove the toothpicks before serving.

> Nonstick vegetable oil spray
> 2 cups plain low-fat yogurt
> 2 cups kasha
> 1 medium egg, slightly beaten
> Salt and pepper to taste
> 2 tablespoons whipped butter *or* diet margarine
> 1 medium onion, finely chopped
> ½ pound mushrooms, scrubbed, trimmed, and finely chopped
> 6 very thin "breakfast" porterhouse steaks (10 ounces total weight), lean meat only
> ⅓ cup canned condensed beef consommé, diluted with ⅓ cup water
> Chopped fresh dill (optional)

Prepare a small casserole or baking dish by spraying the bottom and sides with nonstick vegetable oil. Set aside.

Line a strainer with a double thickness of cheesecloth. Pour in the yogurt and drain for 30 minutes. Reserve.

Combine the kasha and egg and cook according to package directions. Add the salt and pepper.

Melt 1 tablespoon butter in a nonstick skillet. Add the onions and mushrooms and sauté until soft. Add to the kasha and mix thoroughly. Reserve.

Add the remaining tablespoon of butter to the skillet and brown the steaks on both sides.

Spread two thirds of the kasha on the bottom of the prepared casserole. Divide the remaining kasha into 6 equal portions. Place one portion in the center of each steak, roll it up, and secure with a toothpick. Arrange the steak rolls on top of the kasha in the casserole.

Combine the beef consommé and yogurt and pour it over the meat. Cover and bake 20 minutes in a preheated 350°F oven. Remove the cover and bake an additional 15 minutes or until the meat is quite tender. Garnish with dill.

*Yield: 6 diet servings*
*Calories per serving: 326*

---

### STUFFED BEEFSTEAK MENU PLAN

*906 Calories (plus 200-calorie snack)*

Coffee, tea, or noncaloric beverages as desired

## BREAKFAST

1 cup plain low-fat yogurt
¾ cup fresh or unsweetened frozen strawberries
1 tablespoon wheat germ

(*Substitute:* Basic Breakfast 1)

## LUNCH

Turkey Salad
  2 ounces turkey
  1 small tomato, chopped
  1 cucumber, chopped
  1 scallion, chopped (optional)
  1 teaspoon mustard *or* diet mayonnaise
1 1-ounce whole wheat bread pocket
1 cup skim milk

(*Substitute:* Basic Lunch 3)

## DINNER

1 diet serving Stuffed Beefsteak
1 serving Super Spinach Salad

## Kasha Queen Kristina

To prepare this recipe ahead, arrange everything except the consommé and orange juice in the casserole and refrigerate.

Nonstick vegetable oil spray
1 cup kasha
1 medium egg
6 thin veal cutlets (12 ounces)
1 teaspoon salt
¼ teaspoon freshly ground black pepper
½ teaspoon sugar
1 ounce Parmesan cheese, finely grated
2 tablespoons whipped butter *or* diet margarine
4 large carrots, scraped and thinly sliced
Grated rind of 1 orange
2 medium navel oranges, peeled and thickly sliced
1 cup canned condensed beef consommé, diluted
    with 1 cup water
4 tablespoons freshly squeezed orange juice
1 tablespoon chopped mint (optional)
Several sprigs fresh mint (optional)

Spray the bottom and sides of a casserole with nonstick vegetable oil. Set aside.

Cook the kasha and egg in a heavy, dry skillet until the grains are coated. Turn it into the baking dish and reserve.

Lay the cutlets between two sheets of wax paper and pound until very thin.

Combine the salt, pepper, sugar, and cheese and sprinkle over the cutlets.

Melt the butter in a large nonstick skillet; add the cutlets and brown quickly on both sides.

Lay the cutlets side by side, but not touching, on top of the kasha in the baking dish. Cover the cutlets with the carrot slices. Sprinkle the grated rind over the carrots and cover with the orange slices.

Pour in the beef consommé, cover, and bake 30 minutes in a preheated 325°F oven. Uncover, add the orange juice, and bake an additional 15 to 20 minutes or until the meat is tender and the liquid has been absorbed.

Sprinkle with the chopped mint and garnish with the mint leaves.

*Yield: 6 diet servings*
*Calories per serving: 316*

---

### KASHA QUEEN KRISTINA MENU PLAN

*908 Calories (plus 200-calorie snack)*
Coffee, tea, or noncaloric beverages as desired

**BREAKFAST** (*Substitute:* Basic Breakfast 1)

½ cup low-fat cottage cheese
¾ cup fresh diced pineapple
1 slice whole wheat toast

**LUNCH** (*Substitute:* Basic Lunch 1)

3 ounces lean chopped beef, broiled, or fried in nonstick pan
½ tomato, sliced
2 lettuce leaves
2 slices whole wheat bread
½ cup skim milk

**DINNER**

1 diet serving Kasha Queen Kristina
1 cup skim milk

## Midwinter Casserole

This hearty and filling casserole is perfect for cold winter nights when the body craves carbohydrates.

### Sauce

2 tablespoons whipped butter *or* diet margarine
1 tablespoon flour
⅓ cup prepared canned beef consommé
3 medium onions, finely chopped
1 clove garlic, finely chopped
2 tablespoons tomato paste
1 tablespoon red wine vinegar
Pinch salt and pepper

### Casserole

Nonstick vegetable oil spray
1 cup kasha
3 beef bouillon cubes, in 2 cups boiling water
6 ounces very lean lamb, ground
¼ pound fresh mushrooms, thinly sliced
1 teaspoon salt
1 tablespoon finely chopped dill
1 tablespoon finely chopped parsley
½ pound potatoes, peeled, boiled, and mashed

Spray bottom and sides of a casserole with nonstick vegetable oil.

Melt 1 tablespoon butter in a nonstick saucepan. Sprinkle with flour and slowly add the consommé. Stir until smooth. Remove from the heat.

Melt the remaining butter in a nonstick skillet. Add the onions and garlic and sauté, stirring until soft. Add the tomato paste, vinegar, salt, and pepper; stir and cook 5 minutes. Add the consommé and simmer 5 minutes. Turn into a blender and purée.

Prepare the kasha according to package directions, omitting the egg and substituting the bouillon for water.

Brown the lamb lightly in a nonstick skillet. Add the mushrooms and cook, stirring occasionally, until they release their liquid. Sprinkle with the salt, dill, and parsley and mix.

Combine the meat and potatoes in a bowl; add the kasha and half the sauce and mix thoroughly. Correct seasoning.

Turn into the prepared casserole and pour the remaining sauce over the top. Bake in a preheated 350°F oven for 15 minutes.

*Yield: 4 diet servings*
*Calories per serving: 304*

---

### MIDWINTER CASSEROLE MENU PLAN

*897 Calories (plus 200-calorie snack)*
Coffee, tea, or noncaloric beverages as desired

**BREAKFAST**       (*Substitute:* Basic Breakfast 2)

    1 bran muffin
    1 tablespoon diet jelly
    1 cup skim milk

**LUNCH**      (*Substitute:* Basic Lunch 1)

    Tuna Pocket
        3½ ounces water-packed tuna
        ½ cucumber, chopped
        1 scallion, chopped (optional)
        1 tablespoon diet mayonnaise
        1 1-ounce whole wheat bread pocket
    ½ cup skim milk

**DINNER**

    1 diet serving Midwinter Casserole
    ½ cup skim milk

## Ukrainian Lamb

Unlike other Russian food, Ukrainian food is sometimes lightly spiced. If you find this dish too bland for your taste, pass a pepper mill around the table with it.

2 cups kasha
5 cubes beef bouillon, dissolved in 4 cups boiling water
2 tablespoons whipped butter *or* diet margarine
1 onion, finely chopped
¼ pound fresh mushrooms, thinly sliced
6 ounces very lean lamb, ground
Nonstick vegetable oil spray
1 teaspoon salt
1 tablespoon finely chopped parsley
1 tablespoon chopped fresh dill *or* 2 teaspoons dried

Cook the kasha according to the package directions, omitting the egg and substituting the bouillon for water.

Melt 1 tablespoon butter in a nonstick skillet. Add the onion and mushrooms and sauté until soft. Add the lamb and cook, stirring, until all the meat is brown. Set aside.

Prepare a casserole or baking dish by spraying the bottom and sides lightly with nonstick vegetable oil. Set aside until needed.

Combine the meat mix, kasha, and salt in a bowl. Turn into the prepared casserole and bake 10 minutes in a preheated 325°F oven. Sprinkle with parsley and dill and dot with remaining butter.

Serve immediately.

*Yield: 4 diet servings*
*Calories per serving: 339*

## UKRAINIAN LAMB MENU PLAN

*895 Calories (plus 200-calorie snack)*

Coffee, tea, or noncaloric beverages as desired

### BREAKFAST

½ cup fresh or unsweetened frozen strawberries
½ cup cut-up cantaloupe
1 cup plain low-fat yogurt
1 teaspoon wheat germ

(*Substitute:* Basic Breakfast 1)

### LUNCH

Turkey on the Round
   1 bagel, plain or toasted
   2 ounces cooked turkey
   Romaine lettuce leaves
   1 teaspoon diet mayonnaise *or* mustard
½ cup skim milk

(*Substitute:* Basic Lunch 1)

### DINNER

1 diet serving Ukrainian Lamb
½ cup skim milk

*◆§ At a dinner party, eat very, very slowly. That way, there will be food on your plate when the seconds are passed, and you won't be offered any.*

## Spinach-and-Crab

This dish can't be prepared in advance. But don't despair — a quick glance at the recipe will prove how easy it is to put together.

> 2 tablespoons whipped butter *or* diet margarine
> 10 scallions, white and green parts, trimmed and finely chopped
> 2 cloves garlic, finely minced
> 4 tablespoons Sour Half-and-Half (page 28)
> 2 tablespoons flour
> 1 cup evaporated low-fat milk
> 3 packages frozen chopped spinach, cooked and drained thoroughly
> 24 ounces crab meat, drained, picked over, and flaked
> 2 tablespoons grated Parmesan cheese
> Salt, pepper, and mace to taste
> 2 cups kasha, cooked in canned chicken broth instead of water, according to the package directions

Melt the butter in a nonstick saucepan. Add the scallions and garlic and sauté until soft. Add the half-and-half and stir, sprinkling in the flour. Continue stirring while slowly adding the milk. Cook, stirring, until the sauce thickens slightly.

Combine the spinach, crab meat, and cheese and mix. Taste and add the salt, pepper, and mace. Turn the spinach mixture into the saucepan and mix gently but thoroughly.

Arrange the cooked kasha on a serving platter and pour the spinach and crab over it.

*Yield: 6 diet servings*
*Calories per serving: 420*

## SPINACH-AND-CRAB MENU PLAN

*918 Calories (plus 200-calorie snack)*

Coffee, tea, or noncaloric beverages as desired

### BREAKFAST

1 cup bran flakes
1 tablespoon raisins
1 cup skim milk

(*Substitute:* Basic Breakfast 1)

### LUNCH

Vegetable Tostada
2 frozen corn tortillas, heated in nonstick
  pan
½ cup shredded romaine lettuce
1 scallion, chopped (optional)
½ cucumber, chopped
1 green pepper, chopped
1 cup low-fat cottage cheese
Chopped chili peppers *or* salsa to taste

(*Substitute:* Basic Lunch 2)

### DINNER

1 diet serving Spinach-and-Crab

❧ *The waitress is not your mother. She
doesn't care whether you clean your
plate at the restaurant.*

## *Tabbouleh*

A variation of this refreshing and filling salad is served in all countries of the Middle East. Our particular version is considerably lower in fat than the traditional recipe, but its flavor is in no way diminished.

This salad must be prepared at least 24 hours before serving.

> 8 ounces bulgur
> 4 beef bouillon cubes, dissolved in 4 cups boiling water
> 2 medium onions, chopped
> 2 large tomatoes, peeled, seeded, and coarsely chopped
> 2 tablespoons fresh chopped mint, or 1 tablespoon dried
> ½ cup chopped parsley
> 2 tablespoons olive oil
> 4 tablespoons freshly squeezed lemon juice
> 2 tablespoons warm water
> ½ teaspoon coarse salt

Put the bulgur into a flat bowl or basin and pour the boiling bouillon over it. Let it soak for 30 minutes.

Line a colander or large strainer with a clean dish towel. Pour the soaked bulgur into the towel and drain. Squeeze out as much liquid as possible and turn the bulgur into an attractive serving bowl.

Add the onions, tomatoes, mint, and parsley. Toss to mix thoroughly.

Whisk the oil, juice, water, and salt together in a small bowl. Pour over the bulgur and toss until the dressing is completely absorbed.

Refrigerate overnight.

Serve on a bed of lettuce or cabbage.

> *Yield: 6 diet servings*
> *Calories per serving: 209*

## *TABBOULEH MENU PLAN*

*890 Calories (plus 200-calorie snack)*

Coffee, tea, or noncaloric beverages as desired

### BREAKFAST

1 cup vanilla-flavored low-fat yogurt
1 tablespoon wheat germ

(*Substitute:* Basic Breakfast 1)

### LUNCH

3 ounces lean chopped beef, broiled, or fried in
nonstick pan
1 tomato, sliced
1 green pepper, chopped
1 slice onion (optional)
Ketchup *or* mustard
1 1-ounce whole wheat bread pocket, toasted
½ cup skim milk

(*Substitute:* Basic Lunch 1)

### DINNER

1 diet serving Tabbouleh
2 ounces broiled lean fish *or* lobster with lemon
slice
1 serving any Super Salad
½ cup skim milk

## *Bulgur Soup*

This dish may be prepared ahead of time and reheated slowly. It should not be frozen because reheated bulgur gets very mushy.

Nonstick vegetable oil spray
½ pound veal loin, trimmed of all fat and cut into
  ½-inch cubes
Salt and pepper to taste
1½ medium onions, quartered
1 large carrot, quartered
1 teaspoon ground cinnamon
½ teaspoon ground cumin
2 cans condensed chicken broth, diluted with
3 cans cold water
1¼ cups bulgur
Warm water
½ tablespoon freshly squeezed lemon juice
3 tablespoons parsley, chopped fine
1 tablespoon finely chopped fresh mint *or* ½ tablespoon dried
Grated rind of 1 lemon

Spray the bottom of a 2-quart saucepan with nonstick vegetable oil and place it over moderately high heat.

Sprinkle the veal lightly with salt and pepper and brown quickly on all sides in the saucepan. Remove from the heat.

Add the onions and carrot and sprinkle with the cinnamon and cumin. Stir to mix.

Add the diluted broth and bring to a boil; reduce the heat, cover, and simmer 1 hour or until the meat is tender.

Meanwhile, soak the bulgur in warm water and lemon juice to cover for 15 minutes and add it to the saucepan when the meat is tender. Simmer 15 minutes longer or until the bulgur is soft.

Combine the parsley, mint, and lemon rind. When the

soup is done, ladle it into serving bowls, sprinkle with the parsley mix, and serve.

*Yield: 6 diet servings*
*Calories per serving: 267*

---

### BULGUR SOUP MENU PLAN

*890 Calories (plus 200-calorie snack)*
Coffee, tea, or noncaloric beverages as desired

### BREAKFAST

1 bagel, toasted
¼ cup low-fat cottage cheese

(*Substitute:* Basic Breakfast 4)

### LUNCH

Crunchy Cold-Cut Salad
    4 ounces lean cold cuts, chopped
    1 dill pickle, chopped
    ¼ onion, chopped
    ½ green pepper, chopped
    1 carrot, chopped
    1 tablespoon diet mayonnaise mixed with
      mustard
    1 1-ounce whole wheat bread pocket
    ½ cup skim milk

(*Substitute:* Basic Lunch 1)

### DINNER

1 diet serving Bulgur Soup
½ serving Basic Super Salad
1 cup skim milk

## *Ali Baba Pilaf*

To prepare ahead, assemble the casserole. Cool to room temperature, cover with foil, and refrigerate.

To serve, remove it from the refrigerator and let it return to room temperature. Bake the casserole in a preheated 375 °F oven for 10 minutes or until it bubbles.

Nonstick vegetable oil spray
1 cup bulgur
Cold water
¼ cup white rice
1 tablespoon olive oil
10 ounces very lean leg of lamb, ground
2 onions, finely chopped
2 tablespoons chopped fresh mint *or* 1 tablespoon dried
3 tablespoons chopped parsley
1 teaspoon salt
¼ teaspoon freshly ground black pepper
3 medium tomatoes, peeled and chopped
1½ cups beef broth
2 tablespoons dried currants
2 tablespoons pignolia (pine nuts)

Prepare a medium-sized casserole or baking dish by spraying the bottom and sides with nonstick vegetable oil. Set aside.

Soak the bulgur in cold water for 15 minutes. Drain and squeeze it dry in a clean towel. Mix with the rice and reserve.

Heat the oil in a nonstick skillet. Add the lamb, onions, half the mint, and 1 tablespoon parsley. Sauté, stirring, until the meat is brown and the onions soft.

Pat half the bulgur/rice mix lightly on the bottom of the casserole. Sprinkle a little parsley, mint, salt, and pepper over it. Top this with the meat. Sprinkle with a little salt and pepper and cover with the tomatoes. Sprinkle the remaining salt, pepper, and mint over it.

Toss the remaining parsley with the bulgur/rice and arrange it loosely over the tomatoes. Pour the beef broth over the top; sprinkle with the currants and nuts and bake in a preheated 375°F oven 45 minutes or until it browns and bubbles. Garnish with parsley.

*Yield: 6 diet servings*
*Calories per serving: 297*

---

### ALI BABA PILAF MENU PLAN

*900 Calories (plus 200-calorie snack)*
Coffee, tea, or noncaloric beverages as desired

**BREAKFAST**     (*Substitute:* Basic Breakfast 2)

¾ cup fresh or unsweetened frozen strawberries *or* ½ grapefruit
1 slice whole wheat toast
1 slice skim-milk mozzarella cheese

**LUNCH**     (*Substitute:* Basic Lunch 1)

2 ounces chopped lean beef, broiled, or fried in nonstick pan
1 tomato, sliced
1 slice onion (optional)
1 bagel, toasted
1 cup skim milk

**DINNER**

1 diet serving Ali Baba Pilaf
1 cup broccoli, sprinkled with
Cottage Cheese Sprinkle (page 29; optional)
1 cup skim milk

## Turkish Lamb

Most Americans would agree that this dish tastes best hot, but you may prepare it early and serve it at room temperature, as the Turks would.

> 1 1-pound eggplant
> 1 cup bulgur
> 1 tablespoon flour
> ½ teaspoon garlic salt
> ¼ teaspoon freshly ground black pepper
> 10 ounces very lean leg of lamb, cut in ½-inch cubes
> 1 tablespoon olive oil
> 1 medium onion, very thinly sliced
> 1 medium can peeled tomatoes
> ½ cup dry white wine
> ½ cup water
> 4 tablespoons pignolia (pine nuts; chopped walnuts may be substituted)
> 1 tablespoon whipped butter *or* diet margarine
> Salt and pepper to taste
> Chopped dill for garnish (optional)

Bake the whole eggplant, unpeeled, in a preheated 350°F oven until soft — about 1 hour.

Cook the bulgur according to the directions on the package and keep warm.

Meanwhile, combine the flour, garlic salt, and pepper in a paper bag and shake to mix. Add the lamb and shake to coat.

Heat the oil in a nonstick saucepan. Add the lamb cubes and brown them slightly. Add the onion and sauté, stirring, until it begins to yellow. Stir in the tomatoes, wine, and water. Simmer, covered, 30 minutes, or until the lamb is tender. Add the nuts and cook an additional 5 minutes.

Peel the eggplant and mash it thoroughly in a saucepan over low heat; add the butter and correct the seasoning.

Arrange the mashed eggplant in the center of a serving platter and flatten. Spoon the bulgur in a ring around the eggplant and place the lamb and sauce over the eggplant. Garnish with a sprinkling of chopped dill.

*Yield: 6 diet servings*
*Calories per serving: 313*

---

### *TURKISH LAMB MENU PLAN*

*885 Calories (plus 200-calorie snack)*

Coffee, tea, or noncaloric beverages as desired

**BREAKFAST**

½ cup fresh or unsweetened frozen strawberries
½ cup low-fat cottage cheese, mixed with
¼ cup plain low-fat yogurt
½ English muffin

(*Substitute:* Basic Breakfast 4)

**LUNCH**

Sprouted Eggs
2 hard-boiled eggs, chopped
½ cup chopped green pepper
½ cup alfalfa sprouts
1 scallion, chopped (optional)
1 1-ounce whole wheat bread pocket

(*Substitute:* Basic Lunch 4)

**DINNER**

1 diet serving Turkish Lamb
1 cup skim milk

## Barley-Chicken Bake

The flavor of this chicken bake is enhanced by early preparation. To make it ahead, follow the recipe through the first baking process, but don't add the peas and following ingredients. Set aside and allow to cool to room temperature.

To serve, preheat your oven to 350°F and continue with the recipe, baking 20 rather than 15 minutes longer.

Nonstick vegetable oil spray
6 chicken thighs (about 1½ pounds), all visible fat removed, pricked all over with a fork
½ ounce dried imported mushrooms
¾ cup hot water
1 tablespoon vegetable oil
2 medium onions, chopped
½ pound fresh mushrooms, thinly sliced
½ cup quick cooking pearl barley
1 cup dry white wine
1 cup chicken broth
1 teaspoon freshly squeezed lemon juice
1 package frozen peas
½ teaspoon dried marjoram
1 tablespoon canned chopped pimientos
Salt and pepper to taste

Prepare a casserole or baking dish by spraying the bottom and sides with nonstick vegetable oil. Set aside.

Brown the chicken on all sides under a hot broiler. Transfer to the casserole and keep warm.

Meanwhile, soak the dried mushrooms in ¾ cup hot water for 15 minutes. Drain, reserve the liquid, and set the mushrooms aside. Strain the liquid through a clean handkerchief or wet cheesecloth and set aside.

Heat the oil in a nonstick skillet. Add the onions and fresh mushrooms and sauté until soft. Add the imported mushrooms, barley, and reserved mushroom liquid. Increase the heat and cook, stirring occasionally, until the liquid has cooked out. Turn the vegetables and barley into the casserole.

Combine the wine, broth, and lemon juice, mix, and pour over the chicken in the casserole. Cover and bake 1 hour in a preheated 350°F oven. When the chicken and barley are soft, add the peas and sprinkle with the marjoram and pimientos. Bake 15 minutes longer. Correct seasoning.

*Yield: 6 diet servings*
*Calories per serving: 254*

---

### BARLEY-CHICKEN BAKE MENU PLAN

*889 Calories (plus 200-calorie snack)*

Coffee, tea, or noncaloric beverages as desired

**BREAKFAST**

½ cup low-fat cottage cheese
½ cup unsweetened canned pineapple
1 slice whole wheat toast

(*Substitute:* Basic Breakfast 4)

**LUNCH**

Swiss Cheese Pocket
1 ounce Swiss cheese
1 tomato, sliced
1 1-ounce whole wheat bread pocket
1 cup skim milk

(*Substitute:* Basic Lunch 3)

**DINNER**

1 diet serving Barley-Chicken Bake
1 serving any Super Salad
½ cup skim milk

## *Lah Majoon (Middle Eastern Pizza)*

When you prepare the meat mixture and the sauce in this recipe a day early, you enhance the flavor of the dish.

To serve, reheat the meat mixture and the sauce separately and continue with the recipe.

> 1 tablespoon olive oil
> 10 ounces very lean lamb, very finely ground
> 3 medium onions, finely chopped
> 1½ cups canned tomatoes, drained and finely chopped
> 3 tablespoons finely chopped parsley
> 1 teaspoon salt
> ¼ teaspoon freshly ground black pepper
> ¼ teaspoon ground cumin
> 6 large (about 2-ounces each) bread pockets

Heat the oil in a medium-sized nonstick skillet. Add the lamb and onions and cook, stirring, until the meat is brown and the onions very soft. Using a slotted spoon, transfer the mixture to a bowl, leaving as much juice and oil as possible in the skillet.

Return the skillet to the heat and add the tomatoes, 2 tablespoons parsley, salt, pepper, and cumin. Bring quickly to a boil and cook 30 seconds. Transfer half the tomato sauce to the lamb and mix. Reserve the remaining sauce. Separate the top from the bottom of each bread pocket with a sharp, pointed knife, being careful not to pierce the surface. The tops and bottoms separate more easily when the bread is fresh and has been slightly warmed in the oven.

Divide the lamb mixture into 12 equal portions. Spread one portion over each half bread ("inside" up), starting from the middle and working toward the outside edges. Place on baking sheets and bake 15 to 20 minutes in a preheated 350°F oven (or less if the edges of the bread start to burn).

Heat the remaining sauce.

Allow two Lah Majoons per person; spoon some hot sauce over each and sprinkle with the remaining parsley.

*Yield: 6 diet servings*
*Calories per serving: 247*

---

## LAH MAJOON MENU PLAN

*898 Calories (plus 200-calorie snack)*

Coffee, tea, or noncaloric beverages as desired

**BREAKFAST** (*Substitute:* Basic Breakfast 4)

1 egg, scrambled in nonstick pan, cooked with
1 slice Lite-line cheese
2 slices Melba toast
½ cup skim milk

**LUNCH** (*Substitute:* Basic Lunch 1)

Cold-Cut Salad
1 hard-boiled egg, chopped
2 ounces lean cold cuts, chopped
1 tablespoon diet mayonnaise mixed with
mustard
1 carrot
2 rice cakes
½ cup skim milk

**DINNER**

1 diet serving Lah Majoon
1 serving Super Spinach Salad
1 cup skim milk

## *Florentine Bread Salad*

Originally, this salad was prepared only by peasants; now it is found in all the great restaurants of Florence. It's a lovely way to use up slightly stale bread and is especially refreshing on hot days.

You may prepare it the night before you plan to serve it, but remember that the onion flavor becomes more pronounced the longer it remains in the refrigerator.

Keep this and all other food in the refrigerator well covered.

8 ounces stale Italian bread, coarsely grated
1 medium red onion, coarsely chopped
¼ cup chopped fresh basil *or* 1 tablespoon dried and ¼ cup chopped parsley
3 medium tomatoes, peeled, seeded, and coarsely chopped
¼ cup red wine vinegar, diluted with 2 tablespoons ice water
Salt and freshly ground black pepper to taste
1 cup canned shrimp, drained

Combine the bread, onion, basil, tomatoes, and half the diluted vinegar in an attractive earthenware or glass bowl. Toss well and taste. Correct seasoning with salt and pepper, cover with plastic wrap, and allow to rest 10 minutes. Toss again and add a bit more vinegar. The bread should be moist, but not soaking, with no accumulated liquid at the bottom of the bowl. If the bread is tart enough for your taste but not sufficiently moist, add small amounts of ice water, tossing between additions, until the bread is soft but not mushy.

Taste, correct seasoning if necessary, and chill for several hours.

Add shrimp and toss just before serving.

*Yield: 4 diet servings*
*Calories per serving: 234*

## *FLORENTINE BREAD SALAD MENU PLAN*

*900 Calories (plus 200-calorie snack)*

Coffee, tea, or noncaloric beverages as desired

### BREAKFAST

½ cup fresh or unsweetened frozen blueberries
*or* 1 tablespoon raisins
1 frozen waffle
½ cup low-fat cottage cheese

(*Substitute:* Basic Breakfast 1)

### LUNCH

Ham-Cheese Melt
   2 slices whole wheat bread
   1 slice lean canned ham (1 ounce)
   1 slice tomato
   1 ounce Lite-line cheese
      Melt under broiler.
½ cup skim milk

(*Substitute:* Basic Lunch 1)

### DINNER

1 diet serving Florentine Bread Salad
1 serving Super Spinach Salad
½ cup fresh or unsweetened frozen strawberries
½ cup skim milk

## *Bavarian Casserole*

To shorten preparation time before dinner, follow the recipe through the first baking process, using a casserole that can go right from the refrigerator into a hot oven. Cool and refrigerate.

To serve, return the casserole to a preheated 350°F oven and bake for 15 minutes. Then complete the dish according to the remaining directions.

> Nonstick vegetable oil spray
> 3 slices (12 ounces) canned cured ham, cut in halves
> 4 cups canned or packaged sauerkraut, drained
> ½ teaspoon caraway seeds
> 1 tablespoon brown sugar
> 1½ cups all-purpose flour
> 1 teaspoon baking powder
> 1 teaspoon salt
> ¼ teaspoon finely ground white pepper
> 1 medium egg, slightly beaten

Prepare a shallow casserole or baking dish for which you have a cover by spraying the bottom and sides with nonstick vegetable oil. Arrange the ham slices on the bottom and set aside.

Combine the sauerkraut, caraway, and sugar in a bowl and mix well. Spread on top of the ham in the casserole and bake, covered, 20 minutes in a preheated 350°F oven.

Meanwhile, sift together the flour, baking powder, salt, and pepper. Stir in the egg and mix to moisten all the dry ingredients.

Drop by spoonfuls onto the sauerkraut; cover and continue baking 30 minutes longer.

> *Yield: 4 diet servings*
> *Calories per serving: 357*

## BAVARIAN CASSEROLE MENU PLAN
*899 Calories (plus 200-calorie snack)*

Coffee, tea, or noncaloric beverages as desired

### BREAKFAST

½ cup low-fat cottage cheese
½ cup fresh or unsweetened frozen strawberries
1 slice raisin bread toast

(*Substitute:* Basic Breakfast 1)

### LUNCH

Almost-Pizza
Put under broiler:
1 2-ounce whole wheat bread pocket, split in half and topped with
2 ounces Lite-line cheese
1 green pepper, cut up
1 tomato, sliced
Ketchup, oregano, and basil to taste

(*Substitute:* Basic Lunch 4)

### DINNER

1 diet serving Bavarian Casserole
1 cup skim milk

◆§ *Sip on a very hot beverage during the meal to slow your eating.*

# 8

## Potatoes

### Peasant Stock

In Belgium this soup is a traditional one-dish meal. Its flavor
improves when it is refrigerated and reheated slowly, and it
freezes beautifully.

½ cup well washed and chopped fresh sorrel *or* ½
   cup watercress plus 1 tablespoon freshly squeezed
   lemon juice
½ cup fresh chervil *or* flat leaf parsley
12 leeks, white parts and 1 inch of the green,
   washed well and cut into ½-inch lengths
2 heads Boston lettuce, trimmed, washed well,
   drained, and finely shredded
1 teaspoon coarse salt
½ teaspoon freshly ground black pepper
½ teaspoon dried savory
2 tablespoons instant beef broth
1 can (1 pound 4 ounces) white kidney beans
1 pound medium boiling potatoes, scrubbed, peeled,
   and quartered

Combine the sorrel, chervil, leeks, lettuce, salt, pepper, savory, broth, and beans in a large soup kettle or stockpot.

Add enough water to cover well (at least 8 cups), then add
the potatoes. Bring to a boil, cover, reduce the heat, and simmer 1 hour or until the potatoes are quite tender. Correct
seasoning. Crush the potatoes lightly with a fork.

Ladle into individual bowls and serve.

*Yield: 6 diet servings*
*Calories per serving: 229*

---

### *PEASANT STOCK MENU PLAN*
*898 Calories (plus 200-calorie snack)*

**Coffee, tea, or noncaloric beverages as desired**

## BREAKFAST

¾ cup fresh diced pineapple
½ cup low-fat cottage cheese
1 slice whole wheat toast

(*Substitute:* Basic Breakfast 4)

## LUNCH

Bagel and Turkey
1 bagel, plain or toasted
2 ounces cooked turkey
Romaine lettuce
Diet mayonnaise *or* mustard
½ cup skim milk

(*Substitute:* Basic Lunch 1)

## DINNER

1 diet serving Peasant Stock
1 serving Basic Super Salad
1 cup skim milk

---

## Spinach-Potato Pie

Prepare this vegetable pie the evening you intend to eat it. Cold leftover servings are good the next day.

> 1 tablespoon whipped butter *or* diet margarine
> 3 tablespoons finely chopped shallots
> 2 cups thoroughly washed and chopped fresh spinach
> 2 cups mashed potatoes
> 2 tablespoons chopped chives
> 1 teaspoon coarse salt
> ¼ teaspoon freshly ground black pepper
> ¼ teaspoon nutmeg
> 4 eggs, slightly beaten
> 1½ cups evaporated low-fat milk
> Nonstick vegetable oil spray
> 2 ounces Swiss cheese, finely grated
> 2 ounces cheddar cheese, finely grated

Melt the butter in a nonstick skillet over moderate heat. Sauté the shallots until soft and add the spinach. Stir to mix, cover, and cook about 3 minutes.

Combine the potatoes and chives and mix. Add to the skillet, stir to mix, and cover. Cook 2 minutes.

Turn the vegetables into a blender; add the salt, pepper, nutmeg, and eggs. Blend, turning on and off, until all the ingredients are mixed but not puréed. Continue blending at lowest speed while slowly adding the milk.

Spray a nonstick 9-inch pie pan with nonstick vegetable oil. Turn the vegetables into it. Sprinkle the top with the cheese and bake in a preheated 375°F oven for 25 minutes or until a knife inserted in the center comes out clean.

*Yield: 6 diet servings*
*Calories per serving: 236*

## SPINACH-POTATO PIE MENU PLAN
*895 Calories (plus 200-calorie snack)*

Coffee, tea, or noncaloric beverages as desired

### BREAKFAST
1 slice bread, dipped in
1 beaten egg, sautéed in
1 teaspoon butter and sprinkled with
1 teaspoon cinnamon sugar

(*Substitute:* Basic Breakfast 2)

### LUNCH
½ cup low-fat cottage cheese
1 small banana, sliced
1 corn muffin

(*Substitute:* Basic Lunch 3)

### DINNER
1 diet serving Spinach-Potato Pie
1 serving Basic Super Salad
1 small orange
1 cup skim milk

❧ *There is nothing wrong with interrupting a diet for a while if life becomes complicated or stressful. Mark a future date on your calendar and start again when things calm down.*

## Insalata Capricciosa

This salad tastes even better when it is made the night before it is to be used and chilled in the refrigerator. Don't add the cabbage or garnish with the cheese until serving time.

1 pound potatoes, peeled, cooked, and diced
2 cups fresh or frozen green beans, trimmed, cut into 1-inch pieces, and cooked until just tender
2 cups cauliflower flowerets, cooked until just tender
1½ cups fresh or frozen peas, cooked until just tender
2 small carrots, diced and cooked until just tender
12 asparagus spears, trimmed, pared, cooked until just tender, and cut into quarters
2 cups mung bean sprouts, uncooked
½ cup chopped parsley
⅓ cup tarragon wine vinegar, diluted with 3 table- spoons water
½ tablespoon salt
⅛ teaspoon freshly ground black pepper
⅛ teaspoon paprika
1 package Equal (low-calorie sweetener)
2 tablespoons sunflower *or* safflower oil
4 cups shredded Chinese cabbage *or* 2 cups shred- ded savoy cabbage
6 ounces Lite-line cheese slices, cut into thin strips

Drain all the cooked vegetables very well.

Combine all the vegetables except the cabbage in a large mixing bowl and toss lightly.

Combine the diluted vinegar, salt, pepper, and paprika in a small saucepan. Quickly bring to a boil and remove from the heat. Add the sweetener and stir until it has dissolved. Pour the hot vinegar over the vegetables, cover loosely with a clean dish cloth, and let cool slightly. Sprinkle with the oil and toss. Chill at least 2 hours, tossing 3 or 4 times.

Drain, correct seasoning, and arrange on a bed of cabbage. Garnish with the cheese.

*Yield: 6 diet servings*
*Calories per serving: 253*

---

### INSALATA CAPRICCIOSA MENU PLAN

*898 Calories (plus 200-calorie snack)*

Coffee, tea, or noncaloric beverages as desired

## BREAKFAST

½ cup fresh or unsweetened frozen blueberries
*or* ½ small banana
½ cup vanilla-flavored low-fat yogurt
½ English muffin, toasted

(*Substitute:* Basic Breakfast 3)

## LUNCH

Ham on Rye
2 slices lean canned ham (2 ounces)
2 slices rye bread
Mustard
1 dill pickle
½ cup skim milk

(*Substitute:* Basic Lunch 1)

## DINNER

1 diet serving Insalata Capricciosa
1 serving Super Spinach Salad
1 cup skim milk

# Vegetarian Bake

Leftover Vegetarian Bake is delicious. Reheat it in the oven, adding a little water if necessary to keep it moist.

> 6 leeks (5 inches long), trimmed, washed thoroughly, and chopped
> 1 large parsnip, scraped and diced
> 3 large carrots, scraped and diced
> 1 large purple-top turnip, peeled and diced
> 1 pound potatoes, peeled and diced
> 2 large cloves garlic
> 2 cups shredded savoy cabbage
> 1 stalk celery, diced
> 4 tomatoes, peeled
> 2 tablespoons chopped parsley
> 1 tablespoon coarse salt
> ½ teaspoon white pepper
> ⅛ teaspoon mace
> ½ teaspoon thyme
> 1 cup dry white wine
> 10 ounces frozen baby lima beans, thawed

Combine all the vegetables, spices, and herbs in a large bowl and toss to mix.

Transfer to a large casserole or baking dish for which you have a cover. Add the wine, cover, and place on a baking sheet in a preheated 350°F oven. Bake 1 hour. Add a little water to moisten, if necessary, and bake an additional 30 minutes.

Uncover, stir in the lima beans, cover, and return to the oven for 30 minutes longer. Taste and correct seasoning.

*Yield: 6 diet servings*
*Calories per serving: 229*

## *VEGETARIAN BAKE MENU PLAN*

*900 Calories (plus 200-calorie snack)*

Coffee, tea, or noncaloric beverages as desired

**BREAKFAST**

½ cup fresh or unsweetened frozen strawberries
½ cup low-fat cottage cheese
1 slice frozen French toast, heated

(*Substitute:* Basic Breakfast 1)

**LUNCH**

Salade Niçoise
1 cup shredded romaine or loose-leafed lettuce
1 hard-boiled egg
2 ounces water-packed tuna
1 ounce ripe black olives
2 slices tomato
1 or 2 slices red onion (optional)
Diet salad dressing
1 rice cake
½ cup skim milk

(*Substitute:* Basic Lunch 1)

**DINNER**

1 diet serving Vegetarian Bake
½ serving any Super Salad
1 small tangerine
1 cup skim milk

## *Potato Surprise*

This dish offers a double reward for your efforts. First, its
unique and delicious flavor will delight you and second, it
may be prepared and assembled ahead of time and baked just
before serving.

> Nonstick vegetable oil spray
> 1 slice lean cured bacon, finely chopped
> 1 large onion, finely chopped
> 1½ pounds potatoes, peeled, cooked, and mashed
> ¼ cup buttermilk
> Salt, pepper, and nutmeg to taste
> 1 cup low-fat cottage cheese
> 4 ounces blue cheese, crumbled
> 8 canned water chestnuts, drained and chopped
> 1 teaspoon salt
> ½ teaspoon freshly ground black pepper
> 1 tablespoon whipped butter *or* diet margarine,
>     melted
> Paprika

Prepare a medium-sized baking dish or casserole by spraying
the bottom and sides with nonstick vegetable oil. Set aside.

Cook the bacon in a nonstick skillet until brown and crisp.
Remove the bacon to a plate, leaving as much as possible of
the rendered fat in the skillet. Heat the fat and add the onion.
Sauté until soft but not brown. Remove and combine
with the bacon. Cool slightly.

Whip the mashed potatoes in a large mixing bowl. Add the
buttermilk and whip again. Beat in the salt, pepper, and nutmeg. Turn half the potatoes into the bottom of the prepared
casserole and smooth with a rubber spatula.

Combine the cheeses, water chestnuts, onion/bacon mix,
salt, and pepper in a small bowl. Mix and gently spread over
the potatoes in the casserole.

Turn the remaining potatoes into the casserole and spread

them evenly to the edges with a spatula. Sprinkle with melted butter and bake 20 minutes in a preheated 350°F oven.

Garnish with a sprinkling of paprika.

> *Yield: 6 diet servings*
> *Calories per serving: 236*

---

### POTATO SURPRISE MENU PLAN

*895 Calories (plus 200-calorie snack)*

Coffee, tea, or noncaloric beverages as desired

**BREAKFAST**     (*Substitute:* Basic Breakfast 4)

1 egg, boiled, or cooked in nonstick pan
1 sausage link
1 slice whole wheat toast
½ cup skim milk

**LUNCH**     (*Substitute:* Basic Lunch 2)

½ cup low-fat cottage cheese
1 tablespoon chopped parsley
1 tablespoon fresh or dried dill
½ cucumber
1 bran muffin, toasted
½ cup skim milk

**DINNER**

1 diet serving Potato Surprise
1 serving Basic Super Salad
1 cup skim milk

---

## *Cheese and Spudcakes*

When you want your dinner preparation to be leisurely, assemble and brown the spudcakes early in the day and refrigerate them. When you are ready to serve, bake them in a preheated 350°F oven for 10 minutes or until they are hot and cooked through.

> 2 cups low-fat cottage cheese
> 3 medium baking potatoes (about 1 pound), peeled, boiled, and mashed
> 1 egg, slightly beaten
> Pinch salt
> 6 tablespoons flour
> 2 tablespoons whipped butter *or* diet margarine
> 2 cups unsweetened applesauce
> 1 teaspoon freshly squeezed lemon juice
> 1 package Equal (low-calorie sweetener) or to taste

Press the cheese through a coarse strainer into a large bowl. Add the potatoes, slightly cooled, the egg, salt, and flour; blend thoroughly. Add a bit more flour if necessary to hold shape. Form into 12 approximately 3-inch-diameter patties.

Melt 1 tablespoon butter in a large nonstick skillet over moderate heat. Rotate the pan to cover the bottom with the melted butter. Add the spudcakes and sauté until crisp. Add the remaining butter, turn the cakes, and repeat.

Place the crisp spudcakes on a nonstick baking sheet and bake 5 minutes in a preheated 325°F oven.

Combine the applesauce, lemon juice, and Equal in a small bowl. Mix thoroughly.

Serve the spudcakes with the applesauce on the side.

*Yield: 4 diet servings*
*Calories per serving: 305*

## CHEESE AND SPUDCAKES MENU PLAN
*900 Calories (plus 200-calorie snack)*

Coffee, tea, or noncaloric beverages as desired

### BREAKFAST
½ grapefruit
½ bagel, toasted
1 slice skim-milk mozzarella cheese

(*Substitute:* Basic Breakfast 3)

### LUNCH
Deli Pocket
    4 ounces lean corned beef
    1 1-ounce whole wheat bread pocket
1 dill pickle
½ cup skim milk

(*Substitute:* Basic Lunch 1)

### DINNER
1 diet serving Cheese and Spudcakes
2 tablespoons Sour Half-and-Half (page 28)
½ serving any Super Salad
½ cup skim milk

*Do your relatives feel hurt if you refuse their food? Tell them you'll have some later. Later can be next year.*

## Egg-in-Potato Casserole

This recipe can easily be divided in half. To freeze it before baking, fill individual casseroles with the hot potato mix and sprinkle them with bread crumbs and cheese, allow them to cool to room temperature, then cover. To serve, bring them back to room temperature and complete the recipe.

> Nonstick vegetable oil spray
> 2½ pounds potatoes, peeled, boiled, and mashed
> ½ teaspoon salt
> 1 tablespoon whipped butter *or* diet margarine, melted
> 3 tablespoons hot buttermilk
> 2 tablespoons seasoned Italian bread crumbs
> 2 ounces Swiss cheese, grated
> 6 medium eggs

Prepare 6 small ovenproof casseroles or bowls by spraying the bottom and sides lightly with nonstick vegetable oil. Set aside.

Combine the hot potatoes, salt, butter, and buttermilk in a heated bowl. Beat with an electric mixer or wooden spoon until smooth.

Divide the potatoes among the 6 casseroles, smooth the tops, and sprinkle with the bread crumbs and cheese.

Bake 10 minutes in a preheated 350°F oven. Remove from the oven.

Using the back of a soup spoon, press a hollow in the top of the potatoes in each casserole. Break 1 egg into each hollow. Bake 5 minutes or until the eggs have cooked.

Serve immediately.

> *Yield: 6 diet servings*
> *Calories per serving: 273*

## *EGG-IN-POTATO CASSEROLE MENU PLAN*

*904 Calories (plus 200-calorie snack)*

Coffee, tea, or noncaloric beverages as desired

**BREAKFAST**

1 small orange
½ English muffin, toasted
1 teaspoon diet jelly
1 cup skim milk

(*Substitute:* Basic Breakfast 4)

**LUNCH**

Ham and Cheese Taco
2 preformed taco shells
2 ounces (2 slices) lean ham, chopped
1 slice Lite-line cheese, shredded
Lettuce, shredded
Salsa to taste
1 cup skim milk
(*Substitute:* Basic Lunch 3)

**DINNER**

1 diet serving Egg-in-Potato Casserole
1 serving Basic Super Salad
1 cup fresh or unsweetened frozen strawberries

***Prolong a meal and your eating time by talking, and make sure you don't talk when your mouth is full.***

## Halloween Chicken Soup

This is a very respectful way to treat your discarded jack-o'-lanterns, provided, of course, they're clean and not plastic. But you don't have to wait for Halloween to make this delicious variation on the old cure-all chicken soup. Try it when you crave a change.

To prepare it ahead of time, follow the recipe through but don't add the spinach. Cool and refrigerate.

To serve, reheat the soup slowly, add the spinach, and cook 1 minute longer.

> 2 tablespoons whipped butter *or* diet margarine
> 2 medium onions, finely chopped
> 1 pound chicken breast, skinned, boned, and all visible fat removed
> 2 pounds pumpkin, peeled, seeded, and cut into 1-inch cubes
> ¾ pound sweet potatoes, peeled and diced
> 2½ cans condensed chicken broth, diluted with 2½ cans water
> ⅛ teaspoon mace
> Grated rind of ½ orange
> ½ pound fresh spinach, washed very thoroughly and coarsely chopped
> Pinch nutmeg
> Salt and freshly ground black pepper to taste

Melt the butter in a 3-quart stockpot or saucepan. Add the onions and sauté until soft. Cut the chicken into bite-sized pieces and add to the onion. Cook, stirring occasionally, about 3 minutes. Do not allow the onions to brown.

Add the pumpkin, sweet potatoes, broth, mace, and orange rind. Bring to a boil, reduce heat, and cover. Simmer about 20 minutes or until the vegetables are tender.

Stir in the spinach and nutmeg. Correct seasoning with salt and pepper, cook 1 minute longer, and serve.

*Yield: 6 diet servings*
*Calories per serving: 248*

---

### HALLOWEEN CHICKEN SOUP MENU PLAN

*898 Calories (plus 200-calorie snack)*

Coffee, tea, or noncaloric beverages as desired

### BREAKFAST

1 egg, scrambled in nonstick pan, cooked with
1 slice Lite-line cheese
2 slices Melba toast
½ cup skim milk

(*Substitute:* Basic Breakfast 1)

### LUNCH

½ cup low-fat cottage cheese
1 cup fresh or unsweetened frozen strawberries
1 bran muffin

(*Substitute:* Basic Lunch 3)

### DINNER

1 diet serving Halloween Chicken Soup
1 slice rye bread

## Potatoes Mont-Doré

Prepare this dish just before you intend to eat it. The potatoes lose their lightness if kept too long.

>Nonstick vegetable oil spray
>1½ pounds potatoes, peeled and quartered
>1¼ cups low-fat milk
>2 egg whites, beaten until stiff but not dry
>1 tablespoon whipped butter *or* diet margarine
>4 inner stalks celery with leaves, finely chopped
>1 medium onion, chopped
>1 pound mushrooms, scrubbed and chopped
>6 ounces cooked frozen (thawed) or leftover
>  chicken, diced
>½ teaspoon salt
>¼ teaspoon freshly ground black pepper
>2 cloves garlic, minced
>1½ tablespoons cornstarch
>2 tablespoons chopped parsley
>1½ teaspoons dried thyme
>1 tablespoon lemon juice
>Salt and freshly ground pepper to taste
>2 ounces imported Swiss cheese, grated

Prepare a deep baking dish or casserole by spraying the bottom and sides with nonstick vegetable oil.

Boil the potatoes until tender. Drain them and mash well or put through a potato ricer. Add 6 tablespoons milk and beat until smooth. Fold the egg whites gently into the potatoes. Reserve.

Melt the butter in a large saucepan. Add the celery and onions and sauté over moderate heat until the onion is transparent. Add the mushrooms, chicken, salt, pepper, and garlic. Cook, stirring occasionally, about 5 minutes.

Soften the cornstarch in 3 tablespoons milk. Add the remaining milk and blend well. Stir the milk into the mushroom/chicken mix. Add the parsley, thyme, lemon juice, salt, and pepper and cook gently an additional 5 minutes to thicken sauce. Correct seasoning.

Turn into the prepared baking dish; heap the whipped potatoes on top and sprinkle with the cheese.

Bake in preheated 375°F oven 20 minutes or until golden brown. Do not allow the cheese to burn.

*Yield: 4 diet servings*
*Calories per serving: 368*

---

### POTATOES MONT-DORÉ MENU PLAN

*923 Calories (plus 200-calorie snack)*

Coffee, tea, or noncaloric beverages as desired

### BREAKFAST

1 cup coffee-flavored low-fat yogurt
1 tablespoon wheat germ

(*Substitute:* Basic Breakfast 1)

### LUNCH

Muenster Pocket
2 ounces Muenster cheese
1 green pepper, chopped
Alfalfa sprouts to taste
1 1-ounce whole wheat bread pocket

(*Substitute:* Basic Lunch 4)

### DINNER

1 diet serving Potatoes Mont-Doré
1 small orange

# *Djuvitch*

Balkan peasants have prepared this traditional vegetable
stew for centuries. On special occasions they add meat or
fish. We have added chicken. Freeze individual diet servings.

Nonstick vegetable oil spray
6 small chicken thighs, skinned
½ teaspoon garlic salt
¼ teaspoon paprika
1 tablespoon olive oil
2 medium onions, finely diced
3 cloves garlic, finely diced
1 large sweet green pepper, finely diced
1 pound potatoes, peeled and diced
½ teaspoon dried rosemary
1 teaspoon coarse salt
¼ teaspoon freshly ground black pepper
4 medium tomatoes, peeled and sliced
½ cup brown rice
¾ cup canned condensed chicken broth, diluted
  with ¾ cup water
¼ cup dry white wine
¼ cup chopped parsley
Paprika

Prepare a covered casserole by spraying the bottom and sides
with nonstick vegetable oil. Set aside.

Sprinkle the chicken with the garlic salt and paprika.
Brown on both sides under a preheated broiler. Remove the
bone and cut the chicken into 1-inch cubes. Set aside.

Heat the olive oil in a nonstick skillet. Add onions, garlic,
and green pepper. Sauté, stirring until soft. Remove with a
slotted spoon and reserve. Add the potatoes and brown
slightly.

Combine the rosemary, salt, and pepper.

Layer the food in the casserole, sprinkling the seasoning
after each addition, in the following order: onion/pepper

mix, half the tomatoes, potatoes, rice, remaining tomatoes, chicken.

Pour the broth and wine into the casserole. Cover and bake in a preheated 325°F oven until all the liquid is absorbed — 1 hour or more. Sprinkle with parsley and paprika.

*Yield: 6 diet servings*
*Calories per serving: 261*

---

### DJUVITCH MENU PLAN

*887 Calories (plus 200-calorie snack)*
Coffee, tea, or noncaloric beverages as desired

**BREAKFAST** *(Substitute:* Basic Breakfast 4)

French Toast
    1 slice bread, dipped in
    1 beaten egg, sautéed in
    1 teaspoon butter
¼ cup low-fat cottage cheese

**LUNCH** *(Substitute:* Basic Lunch 1)

2 taco shells, filled with
    3 ounces chopped lean beef, broiled
    1 tomato, chopped
    1 green pepper, chopped
    ½ onion, chopped
    Lettuce
    Salsa to taste
½ cup skim milk

**DINNER**

1 diet serving Djuvitch
½ serving any Super Salad
½ cup fresh or unsweetened frozen strawberries

## Curried Veal

An English wit once wrote that anything can go into a curry: old shoes, old hats, even old gloves.

There are no such exotic ingredients in our curry, but you'll enjoy the richness of flavor that comes from the combination of meat, fruit, vegetables, and spices. Cook this stew just before serving to get the maximum taste from it. To reheat leftovers, add a little water to the bottom of the pan and heat gently.

2 cucumbers
½ teaspoon salt
1 tablespoon whipped butter *or* diet margarine
2 medium onions, chopped
6 very thin veal cutlets (12 ounces)
2 medium tart apples, peeled, cored, and coarsely chopped
¼ cup unsweetened apple juice
1 tablespoon curry powder (less for a milder flavor)
2 teaspoons flour
½ cup canned condensed chicken broth, diluted with ½ cup water
1¼ pounds potatoes, peeled, boiled, and cubed
3 tablespoons freshly squeezed lemon juice
Salt and pepper to taste
¼ cup plain low-fat yogurt
Chopped coriander or dill (optional)

Peel the cucumber, cut in half lengthwise, and scoop out the seeds with a small spoon. Chop coarsely, put in a colander or strainer, sprinkle with salt, and let drain for 10 minutes.

Meanwhile, melt the butter in a nonstick skillet. Add the onions and sauté until soft. Remove from the pan and add the cutlets. Brown quickly on both sides and remove to a heated platter. Cut into ¼-inch strips.

Return the onions to the skillet and add the apples and juice. Cover and simmer gently until the apples are tender but not soft. Sprinkle with the curry and flour and blend well. Add the broth slowly, stirring until smooth. Return the meat and add the potatoes. Cook 10 minutes, stirring occasionally. Stir in the lemon juice and add salt and pepper.

Place the cucumbers in a small bowl. Add the yogurt and mix. Garnish with fresh coriander or dill.

Serve the curry with the cucumbers on the side.

*Yield: 6 diet servings*
*Calories per serving: 271*

---

## CURRIED VEAL MENU PLAN

*901 Calories (plus 200-calorie snack)*

**Coffee, tea, or noncaloric beverages as desired**

### BREAKFAST

1 cup cooked oatmeal
1 tablespoon raisins
½ cup skim milk

(*Substitute:* Basic Breakfast 3)

### LUNCH

Cheese-Rice Cakes
2 rice cakes
2 ounces skim-milk mozzarella cheese
1 cup skim milk

(*Substitute:* Basic Lunch 3)

### DINNER

1 diet serving Curried Veal
1 serving Basic Super Salad
½ cup skim milk

## Skier's Choice

This hearty meal is a favorite of skiers all over Austria, Germany, and Switzerland, and no wonder. After a hard day of skiing there's no pleasanter way to restore one's energy than by tackling a steaming plateful of sausage and potatoes with sauerkraut.

Prepare this dish ahead of time and you'll find it's even tastier than when eaten immediately after cooking. Remember to cool it to room temperature before refrigerating. To serve, reheat it slowly until it bubbles.

> Nonstick vegetable oil spray
> 1 slice (1 ounce) cured bacon, finely chopped
> 3 medium onions, finely diced
> 1 carrot, scraped and minced
> 2 pounds canned sauerkraut, drained and liquid reserved
> 1 pound potatoes, peeled and diced
> 1 teaspoon salt
> 3 juniper berries
> ½ cup dry white wine
> 1 small Granny Smith or other tart apple, peeled, cored, and chopped
> 1 teaspoon brown sugar
> 10 ounces knockwurst, quartered lengthwise and sliced

Spray a large nonstick skillet for which you have a cover with nonstick vegetable oil. Sauté the bacon until very brown.

Add the onions and carrot to the skillet and cook until soft. Add the sauerkraut, mix, and sauté 3 minutes. Stir in the potatoes, salt, berries, and wine. Cover and cook over very low heat about 1 hour or until the vegetables are quite soft. Add the reserved sauerkraut liquid if necessary to keep the mixture moist.

When the vegetables are done, add the apple, sugar, and

sausages. Stir to mix, cover, and cook an additional 20 minutes.

*Yield: 6 diet servings*
*Calories per serving: 271*

---

### SKIER'S CHOICE MENU PLAN

*898 Calories (plus 200-calorie snack)*

Coffee, tea, or noncaloric beverages as desired

## BREAKFAST

½ cup fresh or unsweetened frozen blueberries
1 cup plain low-fat yogurt
1 rice cake

(*Substitute:* Basic Breakfast 1)

## LUNCH

Sprouted Egg Salad
2 hard-boiled eggs, chopped
1 scallion, chopped
½ cup alfalfa sprouts
½ cup chopped green pepper
1 tablespoon diet mayonnaise
1 English muffin, toasted

(*Substitute:* Basic Lunch 4)

## DINNER

1 diet serving Skier's Choice
½ serving Super Spinach Salad
1 cup skim milk

## *Sole with New Potatoes*

If you measure and assemble all the ingredients for this lovely fish dish ahead, it shouldn't take any longer to prepare than the time it takes to boil the potatoes.

½ cup dry white wine
¼ cup water
¼ teaspoon salt
1 teaspoon plus 2 tablespoons freshly squeezed
    lemon juice
6 fillets of sole (2 pounds)
1 tablespoon cornstarch
1 tablespoon evaporated low-fat milk
2 egg yolks, slightly beaten
½ teaspoon sugar
Salt and white pepper to taste
1 tablespoon chopped dill
2 pounds small new *or* red potatoes, scrubbed well
    and boiled in their skins

Combine the wine, water, salt, and 1 teaspoon lemon juice in a skillet or pan large enough to hold all the fillets in one layer. Bring to a boil, reduce the heat, and simmer 3 minutes. Place the fillets carefully in the pan and poach, covered, 3 minutes or until opaque.

Remove the fillets, very carefully, to an ovenproof serving platter. Set aside but keep warm. Reserve the liquid.

Soften the cornstarch in the remaining lemon juice. Add the milk and mix thoroughly. Stir the cornstarch into the fish liquid, bring to a boil, stirring continually, and cook until it just begins to thicken.

Stir ¼ cup hot liquid into the egg yolks and stir this into the sauce. Add the sugar and season with the salt and pepper. Cook, stirring, until the sauce thickens to the consistency of heavy cream.

Use a paper towel to blot up any liquid that may have collected around the fillets in the serving platter. Spoon the sauce over the fish and set the platter under a preheated broiler for two minutes. Sprinkle the fish with the dill and serve with the boiled potatoes.

*Yield: 6 diet servings*
*Calories per serving: 250*

---

### SOLE WITH NEW POTATOES MENU PLAN

*884 Calories (plus 200-calorie snack)*

Coffee, tea, or noncaloric beverages as desired

**BREAKFAST**

> 1 slice frozen French toast, heated
> 1 poached egg
> ½ cup skim milk
>
> (*Substitute:* Basic Breakfast 4)

**LUNCH**

> Wry Cheese
> 2 ounces Lite-line cheese
> 2 slices rye toast
> Mustard *or* 1 tablespoon diet margarine *or*
> diet mayonnaise
> ½ cup skim milk
>
> (*Substitute:* Basic Lunch 2)

**DINNER**

> 1 diet serving Sole with New Potatoes
> 1 serving any Super Salad
> 1 cup fresh or unsweetened frozen strawberries

## *Halibut and Potato Casserole*

Prepare this casserole just before you intend to eat it.

> Nonstick vegetable oil spray
> 1½ pounds potatoes, peeled
> 2 cloves garlic, bruised
> Salt and pepper to taste
> 2 thin slices lemon
> 1 tablespoon lemon juice
> ¾ cup dry white wine
> 1½ cups water
> 1 pound halibut fillet
> 2 tablespoons whipped butter *or* diet margaine
> 2 tablespoons flour
> 1½ cups evaporated low-fat milk
> 1 teaspoon salt
> ⅛ teaspoon mace
> 2 eggs, separated
> 1 teaspoon cold water
> ½ cup buttermilk
> 1 ounce Gruyère or other Swiss cheese, finely grated
> 2 tablespoons chopped parsley

Spray a casserole lightly with nonstick vegetable oil and set aside.

Cook the potatoes with the garlic until soft. Drain and mash them; season to taste.

Combine the lemon and juice, ¼ cup wine, and water in a skillet. Bring to boil, reduce heat, and simmer 2 minutes. Add the fish, cover, and poach until it flakes; transfer it to a platter. Allow it to cool slightly, then shred.

Melt the butter in the skillet, sprinkle with flour, and, stirring, add the milk, remaining wine, salt, and mace. Stir until the mix comes to a boil. Remove from heat and add the fish. Let cool slightly, stirring gently to prevent lumps.

Whisk the egg yolks 1 minute. Continue whisking and add a little hot sauce. Mix the yolks with the fish sauce.

Combine the egg whites with 1 teaspoon very cold water. Beat the whites until they are stiff but not dry. Mash the potatoes again; add some buttermilk to soften them (no more than ½ cup). Fold gently into the egg whites, turn into the casserole, and smooth. Fold the grated cheese into the reserved fish sauce. Pour over the potatoes and place the casserole in a pan of hot water and bake 45 minutes in a preheated 375°F oven. Sprinkle with parsley and serve.

*Yield: 6 diet servings*
*Calories per serving: 304*

---

### HALIBUT AND POTATO CASSEROLE MENU PLAN

*890 Calories (plus 200-calorie snack)*
Coffee, tea, or noncaloric beverages as desired

**BREAKFAST**      (*Substitute:* Basic Breakfast 2)

    1 small orange
    1 medium egg, scrambled in nonstick pan
    1 slice whole wheat toast
    1 tablespoon diet jelly

**LUNCH**      (*Substitute:* Basic Lunch 2)

    Fruit Salad
        1 cup shredded romaine lettuce
        ½ cup low-fat cottage cheese
        1 cup fresh or unsweetened frozen strawberries
        ½ cup plain low-fat yogurt
    3 rice cakes

**DINNER**

    1 diet serving Halibut and Potato Casserole
    1 serving Super Coleslaw

## Bluefish Bonne Femme

This dish tastes good either hot or chilled. Left overnight in the refrigerator, the fish develops a very rich flavor, but don't try to keep it longer than one day.

Nonstick vegetable oil spray
2 Knorr fish bouillon cubes, dissolved in 1 cup boiling water, *or* 1 cup bottled clam juice
4 tablespoons dry sherry
2 thin slices onion
1 small clove garlic, bruised
2 peppercorns, bruised
1 thin slice lemon
1½ pounds small red potatoes, washed thoroughly
1 small shallot, finely minced
1½ tablespoons chopped parsley
⅛ teaspoon powdered ginger or ¼ teaspoon grated
1 pound very fresh bluefish fillet, completely scaled
Salt and freshly ground black pepper to taste
¼ pound fresh mushrooms, cleaned and sliced
2 tablespoons whipped butter *or* diet margarine
2 medium egg yolks

Prepare a shallow baking dish by spraying the bottom and sides with nonstick vegetable oil.

Combine the fish bouillon, sherry, onion, garlic, peppercorns, and lemon in a saucepan. Bring to a boil, reduce the heat, and simmer slowly 20 minutes.

Meanwhile, place the potatoes in a saucepan with water to cover and cook until tender. Drain and keep warm.

Sprinkle the bottom of the prepared baking dish with a mixture of the shallot, 1 teaspoon parsley, and ginger. Pat the fish dry and place it in the baking dish. Sprinkle with salt and pepper and cover with the mushrooms.

Strain the stock and pour it around the fish. Bake in a preheated 350°F oven 20 minutes or until the fish flakes.

Transfer the fish carefully to a serving platter. Keep warm. Transfer the stock to a small saucepan over low heat. Add the butter, stirring to melt. Keep stirring and add the egg yolks. Continue stirring until the sauce thickens.

Pour over the fish and serve with the boiled potatoes tossed with the remaining parsley.

*Yield: 6 diet servings*
*Calories per serving: 251*

---

### BLUEFISH BONNE FEMME MENU PLAN

*906 Calories (plus 200-calorie snack)*

Coffee, tea, or noncaloric beverages as desired

**BREAKFAST** *(Substitute:* Basic Breakfast 4)

1 egg, scrambled in nonstick pan
1 slice skim-milk mozzarella cheese
1 slice whole wheat toast

**LUNCH** *(Substitute:* Basic Lunch 1)

2 frozen corn tortillas, heated in nonstick pan
4 ounces lean cold cuts, heated in nonstick pan
Mustard to taste
1 tomato
1 dill pickle, optional
1 cup skim milk

**DINNER**

1 diet serving Bluefish Bonne Femme
1 serving any Super Salad
1 cup skim milk

## *Salmon Potato Croquettes*

The croquettes may be prepared early in the day and refrigerated. To serve, place them in the prepared baking dish and bake 15 minutes in a preheated very hot (450°F) oven.

Nonstick vegetable oil spray
2 tablespoons whipped butter *or* diet margarine
2 medium onions, finely chopped
1 shallot, finely chopped, *or* 1 tablespoon finely
  chopped scallions
1 pound potatoes, peeled, boiled, and mashed
  smoothly
Salt and freshly ground pepper to taste
1½ cups canned chum salmon, drained, skin and
  bones removed, and flaked
2 eggs, slightly beaten
⅛ teaspoon celery seed
3 tablespoons seasoned bread crumbs, mixed with
  1 ounce Parmesan cheese, finely grated

Prepare a shallow baking dish by spraying the bottom and sides with nonstick vegetable oil. Set aside.

Melt the butter in a nonstick skillet. Add the onions and shallot and sauté until golden. Turn into a bowl with the potatoes and mix thoroughly. Season with salt and pepper. Add the salmon, eggs, and celery seed and mix well. Taste and correct seasoning.

Divide into 12 equal portions. Wet your hands and roll each portion into a ball, then flatten into patties between your palms. Don't make the patties too thin. Dredge in the bread crumb/cheese mix and place in the prepared baking dish.

Bake 10 to 12 minutes in a preheated 450°F oven until quite brown.

*Yield: 6 diet servings*
*Calories per serving: 224*

## SALMON-POTATO CROQUETTES
## MENU PLAN

*903 Calories (plus 200-calorie snack)*

Coffee, tea, or noncaloric drinks as desired

### BREAKFAST

½ cup fresh or unsweetened frozen strawberries
1 slice cooked lean ham
1 slice frozen French toast, heated

(*Substitute:* Basic Breakfast 2)

### LUNCH

1 bagel, toasted
2 slices Lite-line cheese
½ cup skim milk

(*Substitute:* Basic Lunch 4)

### DINNER

1 diet serving Salmon-Potato Croquettes
½ cup cooked broccoli
1 serving any Super Salad
1 cup skim milk

᠁§ *Have club soda and "something" at
a cocktail party and sip it slowly.
Make the next drink club soda and
lime.*

## *Make-Ahead Chowder*

This chowder must be prepared at least 24 hours before serving. You may freeze it in individual portions. To serve, add a little water to the bottom of a small saucepan, add the frozen portion, cover, and cook the chowder over low heat until it is heated through. Stir occasionally to prevent burning.

> 1 pound potatoes, peeled and coarsely diced
> Salt
> 2 cups water
> 2 tablespoons whipped butter *or* diet margarine
> 2 medium onions, finely chopped
> 1 tablespoon flour
> 3 cups low-fat milk, mixed with 4 tablespoons powdered skim milk
> 1 7-ounce can water-packed white tuna, drained and flaked
> ¼ teaspoon whole fennel seed *or* ⅛ teaspoon ground
> ½ teaspoon sugar
> Salt and pepper to taste

Place the potatoes in a medium saucepan, cover with salted water, and cook until tender. Drain and reserve the water.

Melt the butter in a 3-quart saucepan over medium heat. Add the onions and sauté, stirring, until soft. Sprinkle the flour over the onions and mix thoroughly.

Stir in the milk. Add the tuna, potatoes, and the water in which they were cooked. Sprinkle with fennel, sugar, salt, and pepper; stir gently and correct seasoning.

Allow the soup to cool to room temperature, then refrigerate overnight.

> *Yield: 4 diet servings*
> *Calories per serving: 217*

## *MAKE-AHEAD CHOWDER MENU PLAN*

*897 Calories (plus 200-calorie snack)*

Coffee, tea, or noncaloric beverages as desired

### BREAKFAST

½ small banana
1 cup coffee-flavored low-fat yogurt
1 tablespoon wheat germ

(*Substitute:* Basic Breakfast 1)

### LUNCH

Whole Wheat Cheese Sandwich
  2 slices whole wheat bread
  1 ounce Swiss cheese
  Mustard
1 carrot
½ cup skim milk

(*Substitute:* Basic Lunch 1)

### DINNER

Make-Ahead Chowder
1 serving Basic Super Salad

*If you must keep ice cream in the house, store it in the coldest part of the freezer. It will be too hard for you to dip into easily.*

# *Cape Cod Clambake*

Prepare this casserole just before you plan to serve it.

> 1 slice lean bacon, chopped
> 2 medium onions, finely chopped
> 1 shallot, finely chopped
> 1 can baby whole clams, drained (reserve liquid)
> 1½ pounds new potatoes, peeled and boiled
> Nonstick vegetable oil spray
> 1 cup evaporated low-fat milk
> 1 tablespoon cornstarch
> ½ teaspoon salt
> ⅛ teaspoon white pepper
> ⅛ teaspoon thyme
> Pinch nutmeg
> 1 tablespoon whipped butter *or* diet margarine

Sauté the bacon in a medium saucepan until it begins to brown. Add the onions and shallot and cook, stirring, until soft and transparent. Remove from the heat. Add the clams and mix thoroughly. Set aside.

Cut the potatoes into ¼-inch slices. Set aside.

Spray a baking dish with nonstick vegetable oil and arrange one layer of potatoes on the bottom. Sprinkle with one third of the clam mix and cover with a second layer of potatoes. Do this twice more, ending with a layer of potatoes.

Combine the milk and cornstarch in a small saucepan and mix completely. Add the salt, pepper, thyme, and nutmeg and stir to mix. Bring just to a boil over medium heat, stirring continually. Remove from the heat, add the butter, and stir to melt.

Pour this sauce over the potatoes in the baking dish, cover, and bake 20 minutes in a preheated 350°F oven. Remove the cover and bake 5 minutes longer.

> *Yield: 4 diet servings*
> *Calories per serving: 314*

## CAPE COD CLAMBAKE MENU PLAN

*897 Calories (plus 200-calorie snack)*

Coffee, tea, or noncaloric beverages as desired

### BREAKFAST

½ cup orange juice *or* ½ sliced banana
1 cup bran flakes *or* Cheerios
1 cup skim milk

(*Substitute:* Basic Breakfast 1)

### LUNCH

3 ounces lean chopped beef, broiled, or fried in
    nonstick pan
2 rice cakes
½ serving Super Coleslaw
½ cup skim milk

(*Substitute:* Basic Lunch 1)

### DINNER

1 diet serving Cape Cod Clambake
½ serving Super Coleslaw
½ cup skim milk

❧ *You're not responsible for finishing
your hostess's leftovers if she prepared too much food for her dinner
party. Let her worry about it.*

## Crab-Stuffed Potatoes

Plan to prepare these luscious potatoes just before mealtime.

>Vegetable oil
>6 medium baking potatoes, scrubbed and dried
>Salt
>½ cup buttermilk (to keep potatoes moist)
>2 tablespoons whipped butter *or* diet margarine
>2 medium onions, finely chopped
>24 medium mushrooms, finely chopped
>2 cans crab meat, drained and picked over
>Coarse salt and freshly ground black pepper to taste
>1 cup dry sherry
>3 ounces imported Swiss cheese, grated
>2 egg whites, stiffly beaten but not dry

Moisten your hands with a small amount of vegetable oil and rub each potato, coating the skins very lightly to help crisp them. Arrange them on the center rack of a preheated 375°F oven and bake 1 hour or until soft. Cool slightly.

Slice each potato in half lengthwise and scoop out the pulp carefully, taking care not to pierce the skin. Sprinkle each potato shell very lightly with salt and set aside. Mash the pulp, adding buttermilk as necessary, and reserve.

Melt the butter in a nonstick skillet over moderate heat. Add the onions and sauté, stirring, 1 minute. Cover and sauté an additional 15 minutes. Add the mushrooms and sauté another 5 minutes, stirring occasionally. Remove from the stove and stir in the crab meat. Season with salt and pepper.

Return to the stove, increase the heat to high, and stir in the sherry. Cook, stirring, until the wine has boiled out. The mixture in the skillet should be quite dry. Remove from heat and add 1 ounce of cheese. Mix thoroughly. Fold the mashed potatoes into the crab stuffing mix. Correct seasoning.

Fold the egg whites into the remaining cheese and reserve. Divide the stuffing equally and fill the potato shells with the crab/potato mixture. Top each with egg white and bake in a preheated 375°F oven until the topping is lightly browned. Serve immediately.

*Yield: 6 diet servings*
*Calories per serving: 262*

---

### *CRAB-STUFFED POTATOES MENU PLAN*

*888 Calories (plus 200-calorie snack)*

Coffee, tea, or noncaloric beverages as desired

**BREAKFAST**    (*Substitute:* Basic Breakfast 4)

½ banana, sliced
½ cup low-fat cottage cheese, mixed with
¼ cup plain low-fat yogurt
2 Melba toast rounds

**LUNCH**    (*Substitute:* Basic Lunch 2)

Wry Cheese
    2 slices rye toast
    2 ounces Lite-line cheese
    Mustard *or* 1 tablespoon diet margarine *or*
        diet mayonnaise
½ cup skim milk

**DINNER**

1 diet serving Crab-Stuffed Potatoes
⅔ cup cooked broccoli
1 serving any Super Salad
1 cup fresh or unsweetened frozen strawberries

---

# 9

## Peas and Beans

### Bean Soup Parisienne

This classical French white bean puréed soup may be frozen in single-serving containers and reheated when desired. Defrost the soup completely in the refrigerator before reheating.

> 1 dozen small onions, peeled and halved
> 2 cubes beef bouillon, in 12 ounces boiling water
> Nonstick vegetable oil spray
> 1 tablespoon whipped butter *or* diet margarine
> 1 small head Boston or other lettuce, shredded
> ¼ teaspoon dried savory or ½ teaspoon fresh
> 5 cubes beef bouillon, in 4 cups boiling water
> ¼ teaspoon white pepper
> 1 can (1 pound 4 ounces) white kidney beans,
>     puréed with their liquid
> 2 tablespoons chopped chives
> 2 ounces cooked chicken, shredded
> Salt

Combine the onions and 12 ounces bouillon in a 4-quart stockpot or Dutch oven. Cook until the onions are tender.

Spray a skillet with nonstick oil and melt the butter over moderate heat. Add the lettuce and savory and toss until lettuce is just wilted. Add to onions and chop finely. Return the vegetables to the bouillon and place the additional bouillon in the stockpot. Reheat.

Sprinkle the pepper over the beans and mix thoroughly. Add to the stockpot and stir. Reheat and serve or divide into individual portions in freezer containers and cool to room temperature. Cover and freeze. When serving, garnish with chives and chicken.

*Yield: 6 diet servings*
*Calories per serving: 154*

---

### BEAN SOUP PARISIENNE MENU PLAN

*909 Calories (plus 200-calorie snack)*
Coffee, tea, or noncaloric beverages as desired

**BREAKFAST**    (*Substitute:* Basic Breakfast 1)

    2 slices raisin bread toast
    ½ cup low-fat cottage cheese
    1 teaspoon Bran-and-Spice Sprinkle (page 29)

**LUNCH**    (*Substitute:* Basic Lunch 1)

    Cold-Cut Salad
        4 ounces lean cold cuts, chopped
        1 green pepper, chopped
        1 dill pickle, chopped
        ¼ onion, chopped (optional)
        1 tablespoon mustard
        1 1-ounce whole wheat bread pocket
    ½ cup skim milk

**DINNER**

    1 diet serving Bean Soup Parisienne
    1 serving any Super Salad
    1 slice rye toast
    1 small orange
    1 cup skim milk

## Thick White-Bean Soup

Like most thick soups, this one benefits by being prepared a day early and reheated slowly, but it also tastes delicious right after it's cooked.

1½ cups dry white kidney beans
8 cups canned chicken broth
1 tablespoon whipped butter *or* diet margarine
1 slice lean bacon, finely chopped
2 medium onions, finely chopped
2 leeks, white part only, sliced
½ cup dry white wine
3 tablespoons chopped parsley
1 bay leaf
¼ teaspoon dried savory
⅛ teaspoon dried marjoram
1 teaspoon salt

Combine the beans and broth in a 3-quart heavy-bottomed saucepan. Bring to a boil and remove from the heat. Let stand 1 hour.

Melt the butter in a medium-sized skillet; add the bacon and sauté until it begins to brown. Add the onions and leeks and cook, stirring, until soft. Set aside.

Add the vegetables to the beans. Stir in the wine, parsley, bay leaf, savory, marjoram, and salt. Bring to a boil; reduce the heat and simmer, uncovered, 1¾ hours or until the beans are quite soft but not mushy.

Transfer 1½ cups beans and some cooking liquid to a blender jar; purée and return to the saucepan. Simmer an additional 15 minutes. Remove the bay leaf and serve.

*Yield: 6 diet servings*
*Calories per serving: 264*

## THICK WHITE-BEAN SOUP MENU PLAN
*889 Calories (plus 200-calorie snack)*

Coffee, tea, or noncaloric beverages as desired

### BREAKFAST

½ cup unsweetened canned pineapple
½ cup low-fat cottage cheese
1 slice whole wheat toast

(*Substitute:* Basic Breakfast 4)

### LUNCH

2½ ounces chicken
1 serving Super Spinach Salad
1 1-ounce whole wheat bread pocket
½ cup skim milk

(*Substitute:* Basic Lunch 1)

### DINNER

1 diet serving Thick White-Bean Soup
1 rice cake
1 cup skim milk

⋙ *Is eating your major form of enter-
tainment? Substitute other "oral"
activities. Sing in a chorus, play a
wind instrument, join a discussion
group, learn bird calls, join a drama
or debating group.*

## Tex-Mex Chili Soup

If this recipe yields more than you can use in an evening, freeze the leftovers in individual-serving containers and keep them until the next time you yearn for a Tex-Mex dinner.

To reheat, place a little water in the bottom of a small saucepan, turn the frozen soup into it, cover, and cook over low heat, stirring occasionally to prevent burning.

½ tablespoon sunflower *or* safflower oil
8 ounces lean ground beef
1 medium onion, minced
3 inner stalks celery, diced
3 cups canned red kidney beans and their liquid
2 cans condensed beef consommé, diluted in 2½ cups cold water
⅛ teaspoon ground cumin
½ teaspoon allspice
1 teaspoon chili powder
Salt and pepper to taste
1 ounce cheddar cheese, grated

Heat the oil slightly in a heavy-bottomed 3-quart saucepan; add the meat and sauté, stirring, until brown. Add the onions and celery and sauté, stirring, 3 minutes longer.

Combine 1½ cups of beans with 2 cups consommé and add to the saucepan. Stir in the cumin, allspice, and chili. Simmer.

Combine the remaining beans and consommé in a blender jar or food processor with a metal blade and purée. Add the purée to the saucepan and correct seasoning with salt and pepper. Simmer gently 20 minutes, stirring occasionally.

Garnish with the cheese.

*Yield: 6 diet servings*
*Calories per serving: 242*

## *TEX-MEX CHILI SOUP MENU PLAN*

*891 Calories (plus 200-calorie snack)*

Coffee, tea, or noncaloric beverages as desired

## BREAKFAST

1 cup plain low-fat yogurt
½ cup fresh or unsweetened frozen strawberries
1 tablespoon wheat germ

(*Substitute:* Basic Breakfast 1)

## LUNCH

Turkey Club Sandwich
2 slices whole wheat bread
2 ounces sliced turkey
1 tomato, sliced
1 tablespoon soybean "bacon bits"
Romaine lettuce leaves
1 tablespoon diet mayonnaise

(*Substitute:* Basic Lunch 4)

## DINNER

1 diet serving Tex-Mex Chili Soup
1 serving Super Coleslaw
1 cup skim milk

# Red-Bean Soup

This soup is so easy and quick to make it will surely become a favorite of the working Carbohydrate Craver.

Leftovers may be refrigerated or frozen in individual-serving containers. Reheat after thawing.

½ slice lean bacon, diced
1 onion, chopped fine
1 carrot, scraped and chopped fine
1 teaspoon brown sugar
⅛ teaspoon white pepper
½ teaspoon salt
1½ cans red kidney beans with their liquid
2 cans beef consommé (with gelatin), diluted with
2 cans cold water
1 cup evaporated skim milk
Pinch cinnamon
3 tablespoons chopped chives

Brown the bacon lightly in a 3-quart saucepan over medium heat. Add the onion and carrot and cook until soft. Stir in the sugar, pepper, and salt and cook 1 minute longer. Add the beans and their liquid and stir occasionally, bringing the mix just to a boil. Transfer the bean mix to a blender or food processor fitted with a metal blade. Stir in 1 cup of the consommé and purée.

Return the purée to the saucepan and combine with the remaining consommé. Bring to a boil over moderate heat, stirring occasionally.

Meanwhile, combine the milk and cinnamon in a small saucepan and scald. Stir the milk into the purée.

Garnish with chives.

*Yield: 4 diet servings*
*Calories per serving: 317*

## RED-BEAN SOUP MENU PLAN

*904 Calories (plus 200-calorie snack)*

Coffee, tea, or noncaloric beverages as desired

### BREAKFAST

¾ cup fresh or unsweetened frozen strawberries *or* ½ grapefruit
1 slice skim-milk mozzarella cheese
½ English muffin, toasted

(*Substitute:* Basic Breakfast 2)

### LUNCH

Greek Salad
½ serving Super Spinach Salad
2 ounces water-packed tuna
1 ounce feta cheese
1 1-ounce whole wheat bread pocket
½ cup skim milk

(*Substitute:* Basic Lunch 1)

### DINNER

1 diet serving Red-Bean Soup
½ serving Super Spinach Salad
1 cup skim milk

❧ *Eating is not a competitive sport. No
prize is given to the person who fin-
ishes first.*

## Fagioli Pirandello

The half-hour or so it takes to prepare this Italian dinner will be time well spent.

Serve leftovers as a salad by adding a teaspoon or so of Pesto-Seasoned Vinegar Dressing (page 23) to each portion, tossing to mix.

6 anchovy fillets, chopped
2 tablespoons olive oil
1 pound fresh or canned plum tomatoes, peeled and drained
¼ teaspoon salt
⅛ teaspoon freshly ground black pepper
1 cup canned red kidney beans
7 ounces Superoni small pasta of your choice
6 large pitted ripe black olives, chopped
2 tablespoons capers
Generous pinch oregano

Combine the anchovies and oil in a medium-sized saucepan. Cook the anchovies over moderate heat, stirring and mashing with a wooden spoon until they are reduced to a paste.

Place the tomatoes in a bowl and mash with a fork. Add the tomatoes, salt, and pepper to the saucepan and mix. Cook about 15 to 20 minutes, stirring occasionally.

Meanwhile, heat the beans in a bit of their own liquid. Keep warm. Cook the pasta. Drain the beans and the pasta and combine.

Add the olives and capers to the sauce and cook 1 minute longer to heat through. Correct seasoning.

Turn the beans and pasta into a decorative serving bowl. Top with the sauce and sprinkle with the oregano.

Toss the beans, pasta, and sauce at the table. Serve immediately.

*Yield: 4 diet servings*
*Calories per serving: 250*

## *FAGIOLI PIRANDELLO MENU PLAN*
*900 Calories (plus 200-calorie snack)*

Coffee, tea, or noncaloric beverages as desired

### BREAKFAST
½ cup orange juice
½ cup cooked hot cereal
1 cup skim milk

(*Substitute:* Basic Breakfast 1)

### LUNCH
Cucumber Boats
1 large cucumber, seeded and filled with
1 cup low-fat cottage cheese, mixed with
1 tablespoon dry onion soup mix
1 scallion, chopped
½ cup chopped green pepper
1 tablespoon chopped parsley
1 English muffin

(*Substitute:* Basic Lunch 4)

### DINNER
1 diet serving Fagioli Pirandello

*❧ Not sure you're losing weight? Try
on clothes that didn't fit before you
started the diet. Your scale can lie;
clothes rarely do.*

## *Salad Sorrentino*

Chill this salad at least two hours — preferably overnight —
before serving.

> 2 cups canned red kidney beans, drained
> 4 small zucchini, coarsely diced
> ¼ pound fresh green beans, trimmed and cooked
>     until just tender (or 1 cup canned, drained)
> 4 tablespoons chopped parsley
> 2 tablespoons chopped fresh basil (if available)
> 2 tablespoons olive oil
> 1 clove garlic, minced
> 1 cup canned chickpeas, drained
> 2 cloves garlic, bruised
> 1 small sweet red pepper, cut into thin shreds
> 3 anchovy fillets, drained and mashed
> 2 teaspoons capers
> 6 pitted ripe black olives, sliced
> 3 large tomatoes, peeled, seeded, and chopped
> 3 teaspoons pesto or plain red wine vinegar
> 2 tablespoons red wine
> 1 medium bay leaf
> ½ teaspoon oregano
> Salt, pepper, and additional vinegar to taste

Combine the kidney beans, zucchini, green beans, parsley,
and basil in a large mixing bowl. Toss and set aside.

Heat 1 tablespoon oil in a medium-sized nonstick saucepan. Add the minced garlic and sauté 30 seconds. Add the
chickpeas, sauté, stirring, an additional 30 seconds, and remove from the heat. Cool slightly and add the minced garlic
and chickpeas to the vegetables.

Heat the remaining oil with the bruised garlic in a saucepan until the garlic begins to brown. Discard the garlic.

Add the peppers and sauté, stirring constantly, 30 seconds.
Combine the anchovies, capers, olives, tomatoes, vinegar,
wine, bay leaf, and oregano and bring to a boil. Reduce the

heat and simmer 8 minutes. Cool slightly and pour over the vegetables. Toss, taste, and correct seasoning with salt, pepper, and vinegar if desired.

*Yield: 6 diet servings*
*Calories per serving: 229*

---

### SALAD SORRENTINO MENU PLAN

*884 Calories (plus 200-calorie snack)*

Coffee, tea, or noncaloric beverages as desired

#### BREAKFAST

1 cup fortified cereal
1 teaspoon raisins
1 cup skim milk

(*Substitute:* Basic Breakfast 1)

#### LUNCH

Lean Tacos
    2 preformed taco shells
    4 ounces lean cold cuts, shredded
    1 ounce Lite-line cheese, shredded
    ½ cup shredded lettuce
    Salsa and onions to taste
½ cup skim milk

(*Substitute:* Basic Lunch 1)

#### DINNER

1 diet serving Salad Sorrentino
1 serving any Super Salad
1 small orange
½ cup skim milk

## Royal Chicken Salad

Don't try to keep this salad overnight; it tends to get soggy. If these proportions are too much for you and your family, divide the recipe to suit your needs.

>  10 ounces diced cooked frozen (thawed) or leftover
>  cubed chicken
>  ¼ cup canned crab meat, picked over and flaked
>  4 stalks celery, trimmed and coarsely diced
>  4 tablespoons chopped parsley
>  1 tablespoon chopped dill
>  1 carrot, washed, scraped, and shredded
>  1 red pepper, trimmed, seeded, and cut into thin
>  strips
>  1 can (1 pound 4 ounces) white kidney beans
>  4 tablespoons diet mayonnaise
>  4 tablespoons freshly squeezed orange juice
>  1 teaspoon cider vinegar
>  1 scant package Equal (low-calorie sweetener)
>  2 cups finely sliced red cabbage (soft leaves only)

Combine the chicken, crab meat, celery, parsley, dill, carrot, pepper, and beans in a large mixing bowl. Toss and chill in the refrigerator.

Whisk the mayonnaise, orange juice, vinegar, and Equal together in a small bowl. Chill in the refrigerator 1 hour.

Pour the dressing over the salad and toss to cover.

Arrange the cabbage on a decorative serving platter or bowl and turn the salad into the center.

*Yield: 6 diet servings*
*Calories per serving: 267*

## *ROYAL CHICKEN SALAD*

*906 Calories (plus 200-calorie snack)*

Coffee, tea, or noncaloric beverages as desired

## BREAKFAST

1 cup corn flakes
1 tablespoon raisins
1 cup skim milk

(*Substitute:* Basic Breakfast 1)

## LUNCH

Hamburger Pocket
3 ounces lean chopped beef, broiled, or fried
in nonstick pan
1 green pepper, chopped
1 tomato, sliced
Ketchup *or* mustard
1 1-ounce whole wheat bread pocket,
toasted
½ cup skim milk

(*Substitute:* Basic Lunch 1)

## DINNER

1 diet serving Royal Chicken Salad
1 hard roll
½ cup skim milk

## Quick Chili 'n' Beans

While this isn't the traditional way to prepare chili and beans, we think you'll appreciate its simplicity.

The finished dish may be cooled, refrigerated, or frozen and reheated slowly when you wish to serve it.

1 slice lean cured bacon, chopped
2 large onions, sliced
2 cloves garlic, minced
10 ounces very lean ground beef
2 tablespoons flour
2 tablespoons chili powder
1½ cans red kidney beans with their liquid
1 teaspoon salt (or to taste)
½ teaspoon ground cumin
1 can condensed tomato soup
½ cup dry white wine
2 tablespoons chopped fresh coriander

Cook the bacon in a large nonstick skillet over moderate heat. Add the onions and garlic and sauté until soft. Add the beef and cook, stirring it with a wooden spoon to keep it separated, until it is all brown.

Sprinkle the flour and chili over the meat and stir in completely. Add the beans, their liquid, salt, and cumin. Mix. Stir in the soup and wine. Simmer, uncovered, 15 minutes.

If you prefer a thinner sauce, add water during the last 5 minutes. If you like your chili thick, increase the heat and cook, stirring occasionally, until the sauce is the consistency you desire.

Garnish with coriander.

*Yield: 6 diet servings*
*Calories per serving: 286*

## *QUICK CHILI 'N' BEANS MENU PLAN*

*892 Calories (plus 200-calorie snack)*

Coffee, tea, or noncaloric beverages as desired

### BREAKFAST

½ cup grapefruit juice
1 cup Cheerios
1 cup skim milk

(*Substitute:* Basic Breakfast 1)

### LUNCH

Corn-Fed Tuna Salad
    3 ounces water-packed tuna
    1 cucumber, chopped
    1 tablespoon chopped parsley
    1 corn muffin, toasted
½ cup skim milk

(*Substitute:* Basic Lunch 1)

### DINNER

1 diet serving Quick Chili 'n' Beans
½ serving Basic Super Salad
1 cup skim milk

*Are nighttimes nibbling times? Eat
dinner as late as possible and sip on
a noncaloric beverage or suck on a
piece of hard candy after the meal.*

## Lentil-Vegetable Soup

This meal-in-a-bowl blends flavors and textures in a way that should satisfy the most discriminating Carbohydrate Craver. Besides being tasty and filling, it is very easy to prepare and keeps well up to two days in the refrigerator.

2 tablespoons olive or vegetable oil
½ pound tomatoes, coarsely chopped
2 medium onions, chopped
2 small cloves garlic, minced
2 inner stalks celery with leaves, chopped
4 cups vegetable juice cocktail
1 cup water
1 beef bouillon cube, mashed, or 1 teaspoon beef
    bouillon powder
1 cup lentils
½ teaspoon dried thyme or 1½ teaspoons fresh
¼ teaspoon freshly ground black pepper
Dash Tabasco sauce
2 ounces imported Parmesan cheese, grated

Heat the oil in a 3-quart nonstick saucepan. Add the tomatoes, onions, garlic, and celery and sauté until the onions are transparent.

Add the juice, water, and bouillon. Stir and bring to a boil. Reduce the heat; add the lentils, thyme, pepper, and Tabasco sauce. Stir, cover, and simmer 30 minutes or until the lentils are soft.

Correct seasoning and sprinkle with cheese.

*Yield: 6 diet servings*
*Calories per serving: 249*

## *LENTIL-VEGETABLE SOUP MENU PLAN*

*907 Calories (plus 200-calorie snack)*

Coffee, tea, or noncaloric beverages as desired

### BREAKFAST

1 bran muffin
½ cup low-fat cottage cheese
1 tablespoon diet jelly

(*Substitute:* Basic Breakfast 1)

### LUNCH

Sprouted Taco
2 preformed taco shells
2½ ounces chicken, shredded
1 cup loosely packed alfalfa sprouts
1 scallion, chopped
1 tomato, chopped
1 teaspoon diet salad dressing
Salsa to taste
1 cup skim milk

(*Substitute:* Basic Lunch 1)

### DINNER

1 diet serving Lentil-Vegetable Soup
½ serving Basic Super Salad
1 slice whole wheat bread
1 small tangerine
½ cup skim milk

## Braumeister's Soup

Many German dishes are cooked with beer. The alcohol evaporates during cooking, leaving only the full-bodied flavor.

    1 bay leaf
    ½ stick cinnamon, broken in half
    3 whole cloves
    1 cardamon seed *or* ⅛ teaspoon ground
    1 cup dry dark lentils
    Nonstick vegetable oil spray
    1 tablespoon sunflower *or* other vegetable oil
    2 medium onions, cut in half and sliced very thinly
    3 cloves garlic, minced
    1 carrot, scraped and finely chopped
    1 celery stalk, washed, trimmed, and finely chopped
    ½ teaspoon coarse salt
    ¼ teaspoon freshly ground pepper
    5 cups cold water
    1 can beef broth
    12 ounces flat dark beer (domestic)
    7 ounces Polish sausage
    1 tablespoon chopped chives *or* scallions (optional)

Place the bay leaf, cinnamon, cloves, and cardamon in a metal tea ball or in the center of a 5-inch-by-5-inch cheesecloth square, tied with string to make a spice bouquet.

Blanch the lentils in boiling water for 30 seconds. Drain and set aside.

Spray the bottom of a 3- or 4-quart heavy-bottomed stockpot or saucepan with nonstick vegetable oil. Add the oil and heat. Combine the onions, garlic, carrot, and celery, add to the saucepan, and sauté, stirring until the onions are golden.

Stir in the lentils, salt, pepper, spice bag, 4½ cups water, broth, and beer. Increase the heat to high, stir, and bring to a boil. Reduce the heat to moderately low and simmer 40 minutes or until the lentils are tender but not soft.

Meanwhile, put the sausage into a steamer and cook for 20 minutes. Cut the sausage into 18 slices and set aside.

Discard the spice bouquet, add ½ cup water and the sausage slices. Bring the soup back to a simmer, cover, and cook 15 minutes longer. Garnish with a sprinkling of chives.

*Yield: 6 diet servings*
*Calories per serving: 253*

---

### BRAUMEISTER'S SOUP MENU PLAN

*883 Calories (plus 200-calorie snack)*

Coffee, tea, or noncaloric beverages as desired

**BREAKFAST** (*Substitute:* Basic Breakfast 2)

1 cup tomato juice
1 poached egg
1 slice whole wheat toast
1 teaspoon diet margarine

**LUNCH** (*Substitute:* Basic Lunch 2)

Confetti Cottage Cheese
  1 cup low-fat cottage cheese
  1 carrot, chopped
  1 tomato, chopped
  1 tablespoon fresh dill *or* 1 teaspoon dried
  1 tablespoon chopped parsley
2 rice cakes

**DINNER**

1 diet serving Braumeister's Soup
1 serving any Super Salad
1 cup skim milk

## Lentil-Pasta Salad

The blend of flavors in this salad ripens and becomes more pronounced when it is prepared the night before.

4 ounces rotini pasta (or your favorite shape)
1 cup dry dark lentils
8 cups cold water
2 teaspoons salt
10 scallions, white and green parts, trimmed and chopped
5 tablespoons canned chopped pimiento
5 tablespoons chopped sour pickle
5 tablespoons chopped parsley
5 anchovy fillets, drained and chopped
3 tablespoons chopped capers
½ teaspoon dried tarragon *or* 1 teaspoon fresh, chopped
Salt and freshly ground black pepper to taste
6 tablespoons wine vinegar
2 tablespoons freshly squeezed lemon juice
1½ tablespoons olive oil
Lettuce
2 tomatoes, sliced very thin for garnish

Break the rotini in half and cook, drain, and chill.

Combine the lentils, water, and salt in a 3- or 4-quart saucepan. Bring to a boil, reduce heat, and simmer 25 minutes or until tender but not mushy. Add small quantities of water if necessary to keep the lentils covered. Drain and cool.

Combine the lentils and pasta in a chilled metal bowl and toss gently to mix. Set aside.

Mix the scallions, pimientos, pickle, parsley, anchovies, capers and tarragon in a small bowl. Add to the lentils and pasta and toss. Taste and add salt and pepper.

Combine the vinegar and lemon juice and add to the salad.

Toss to moisten completely. Sprinkle with olive oil and toss again.

Arrange a bed of lettuce on a serving platter. Turn the lentils and pasta onto it and ring with tomato slices.

*Yield: 6 diet servings*
*Calories per serving: 255*

---

### *LENTIL-PASTA SALAD MENU PLAN*

*904 Calories (plus 200-calorie snack)*

Coffee, tea, or noncaloric beverages as desired

**BREAKFAST**     (*Substitute:* Basic Breakfast 1)

½ cup fresh or unsweetened frozen strawberries
1 tablespoon wheat germ
1 cup plain low-fat yogurt

**LUNCH**     (*Substitute:* Basic Lunch 4)

Turkey Club
    2 thin slices whole wheat bread
    2 ounces cooked turkey
    1 tomato, sliced
    Romaine lettuce
    1 tablespoon soybean "bacon bits"
    1 tablespoon diet mayonnaise

**DINNER**

1 diet serving Lentil-Pasta Salad
1 serving any Super Salad
1 small tangerine
1 cup skim milk

## *Persian Soup*

This interesting and tasty soup may be refrigerated overnight and reheated slowly without loss of flavor.

> Nonstick vegetable oil spray
> 10 ounces very lean lamb, ground twice
> 1 onion, minced
> 1 small clove garlic, minced
> 3 cups canned chickpeas, drained (reserve liquid)
> 3 cans beef consommé (with gelatin)
> 2 cups water
> 1 teaspoon salt
> Freshly ground pepper to taste
> ½ teaspoon ground cumin
> 2 cups canned plum tomatoes with liquid
> Chopped parsley for garnish

Spray a soup kettle with nonstick vegetable oil. Add the meat, onion, and garlic and brown over moderate heat, stirring continually. Add the chickpeas and stir.

Combine the consommé, water, reserved chickpea liquid, salt, pepper, cumin, and tomatoes.

Stir the combined liquids into the kettle and bring to a boil. Reduce the heat, cover, and simmer 1 hour.

Garnish with parsley.

> *Yield: 6 diet servings*
> *Calories per serving: 245*

&ᛞ *Put a large basket on your bike to use when you do errands. After a few days, what seemed an endless trip to the grocery store or dry cleaner will become a trivial distance.*

## PERSIAN SOUP MENU PLAN

*890 Calories (plus 200-calorie snack)*

Coffee, tea, or noncaloric beverages as desired

### BREAKFAST

½ English muffin, toasted
1 slice cooked lean ham
1 slice Lite-line cheese
½ cup skim milk

(*Substitute:* Basic Breakfast 2)

### LUNCH

Fruit Salad
    1 cup shredded romaine lettuce
    1 cup low-fat cottage cheese
    1 cup cut-up cantaloupe *or* 1 small banana
1 slice whole wheat toast

(*Substitute:* Basic Lunch 2)

### DINNER

1 diet serving Persian Soup
1 serving Basic Super Salad
½ cup skim milk

~§ *If you find your fingers "walking"
toward the peanuts or candy at a
party, walk away — fast.*

## Spicy Sausage Soup

Let the soup cool to room temperature before you refrigerate
it. To serve, reheat it slowly. Don't freeze this dish.

1 slice lean cured bacon, chopped
6 ounces spicy Spanish sausage (chorizo), cut into 12
slices
1 can chickpeas, drained (reserve liquid)
2 cloves garlic, minced
1 large can peeled tomatoes, drained and chopped
(reserve liquid)
½ pound fresh spinach, washed thoroughly, tough
stems removed, and coarsely chopped
1 teaspoon ground cumin
1 teaspoon chili powder
Salt and freshly ground black pepper to taste
10 chicken bouillon cubes, diluted in 5 cups boiling
water
2 yellow corn tortillas

Sauté the bacon until slightly brown in a 4-quart saucepan.
Add the sausage and brown lightly, stirring to prevent burning.

Combine the chickpeas, garlic, tomatoes, spinach, cumin,
chili, salt, and pepper; mix and add to the sausage. Cook,
stirring, 1 minute. Add the bouillon and reserved vegetable
liquids, stir, and bring to a boil. Cover, reduce the heat, and
simmer 1 hour.

Meanwhile, cut each tortilla in half, then into thin slices.
Toast the slices in a warm oven.

Taste the soup, correct seasoning, and garnish with tortilla
strips.

*Yield: 6 diet servings*
*Calories per serving: 263*

*SPICY SAUSAGE SOUP MENU PLAN*

*903 Calories (plus 200-calorie snack)*

Coffee, tea, or noncaloric beverages as desired

**BREAKFAST**

½ cup fresh or unsweetened frozen strawberries
½ cup low-fat cottage cheese
1 slice raisin bread toast

(*Substitute:* Basic Breakfast 1)

**LUNCH**

Tuna Melt
2 ounces water-packed tuna
1 ounce skim-milk mozzarella cheese
2 slices whole wheat bread
Melt under broiler.
½ cup skim milk

(*Substitute:* Basic Lunch 1)

**DINNER**

1 diet serving Spicy Sausage Soup
1 serving Basic Super Salad
1 cup skim milk

◆§ *Have trouble walking past bakeries, pizza shops, ice cream stores, doughnut chains? Change your route.*

## Salade à la Grecque

Prepare this salad in advance so you can chill it well before serving. If you do make it early, don't add the tomatoes and cheese until an hour before you are ready to eat.

½ cup dry white wine
1 tablespoon water
2 tablespoons olive oil
Juice of 2 freshly squeezed lemons
2 cloves garlic, finely minced
1 bay leaf
¼ teaspoon oregano
1 sprig parsley
1 pound small button mushrooms, caps and stems, scrubbed, trimmed, and quartered
1 pound small zucchini, washed, trimmed, and diced in large pieces
12 ounces canned chickpeas, drained
3 medium canned pimientos, coarsely chopped
2 large tomatoes, peeled, seeded, and chopped
1 cup low-fat cottage cheese
3 ounces feta cheese, crumbled
Coarse salt and freshly ground black pepper to taste
Lettuce

Combine the wine, water, oil, juice, garlic, bay leaf, oregano, and parsley in a saucepan. Bring to a boil, reduce the heat to moderate, and cook 5 minutes.

Add the mushrooms and cook 5 minutes longer. Remove the mushrooms with a slotted spoon and reserve in a bowl.

Add the zucchini to the liquid remaining in the saucepan. Cook 5 minutes. Again using a slotted spoon, add the zucchini to the mushrooms. Reserve.

Add the chickpeas to the remaining liquid and cook 5 minutes. Combine the chickpeas and liquid with the reserved vegetables. Add the chopped pimientos and toss well. Chill.

One hour before serving, remove the bay leaf, add the tomatoes, and toss to mix. Refrigerate to chill.

Mix the cottage cheese and feta. Reserve.

Just before serving, drain the vegetables, add the cheese, toss, and serve on a bed of lettuce.

*Yield: 6 diet servings*
*Calories per serving: 256*

---

### SALADE À LA GRECQUE MENU PLAN

*894 Calories (plus 200-calorie snack)*

Coffee, tea, or noncaloric beverages as desired

### BREAKFAST

1 corn muffin
½ cup low-fat cottage cheese
1 tablespoon diet margarine

(*Substitute:* Basic Breakfast 3)

### LUNCH

Tuna Taco Crunch
   2 preformed taco shells
   ½ serving Super Coleslaw
   2 ounces water-packed tuna
   1 hard-boiled egg
   1 tablespoon diet mayonnaise
   ½ cup skim milk

(*Substitute:* Basic Lunch 1)

### DINNER

1 diet serving Salade à la Grecque
½ serving Super Spinach Salad
1 cup skim milk

## Chicken Madeira

It's a tossup as to whether this dish tastes better if made ahead and reheated slowly or prepared just before serving time. Suit yourself. In either case, you'll enjoy it!

2 tablespoons whipped butter *or* diet margarine
1 onion, finely chopped
10 ounces frozen (thawed) cooked or leftover chicken, diced
1 cup canned chickpeas, drained
1 small ripe tomato, peeled, seeded, and chopped
Salt and pepper to taste
2 tablespoons flour
4 tablespoons tomato paste
1 cup canned condensed beef consommé, diluted with 1 cup water
4 teaspoons Madeira wine
2½ cups cooked brown rice

Melt 1 tablespoon butter in a nonstick skillet. Add the onion and sauté, stirring, until tender. Add the chicken, chickpeas, tomato, salt, and pepper and toss. Remove to a small bowl, leaving as much onion as possible in the skillet.

Add the remaining butter to the skillet and melt. Sprinkle in the flour, add the tomato paste, and mix until quite thick. Stir in the consommé and keep stirring until the paste has dissolved.

Return the chicken and chickpeas to the sauce, add the wine, and simmer 5 to 8 minutes to heat through.

Serve over the rice.

*Yield: 6 diet servings*
*Calories per serving: 283*

## *CHICKEN MADEIRA MENU PLAN*

*897 Calories (plus 200-calorie snack)*

Coffee, tea, or noncaloric beverages as desired

## BREAKFAST

1 corn muffin
½ cup plain low-fat yogurt

(*Substitute:* Basic Breakfast 3)

## LUNCH

Vegetable Tostada
2 frozen corn tortillas, heated in a nonstick
pan
½ cup shredded romaine lettuce
1 tomato, chopped
½ cucumber, chopped
1 scallion, chopped (optional)
1 cup low-fat cottage cheese
Salsa to taste

(*Substitute:* Basic Lunch 2)

## DINNER

1 diet serving Chicken Madeira
1 serving any Super Salad
½ cup skim milk

## Chickpeas Jerez

Some like it hot, some like it cold, some like it in the pot one day old! Leftovers are a real treat, hot or cold!

> 1 pound chicken breasts, skinned, boned, and all visible fat removed
> 1 tablespoon flour
> 1 teaspoon coarse salt
> ⅛ teaspoon freshly ground black pepper
> Generous pinch ground cloves
> Generous pinch ground cumin
> ½ teaspoon chili powder
> Nonstick vegetable oil spray
> 1 tablespoon sunflower *or* other vegetable oil
> 2 medium onions, very thinly sliced
> 1 large clove garlic, minced
> 1 green bell pepper, coarsely chopped
> 2 cups canned tomatoes, drained (reserve liquid) and coarsely chopped
> 1½ 16-ounce cans chickpeas, drained
> ½ cup dry sherry
> 14 Spanish (stuffed green) olives, sliced

Cut each chicken breast into thirds. Combine the flour, salt, pepper, cloves, cumin, and chili in a plastic or paper bag. Fold the top securely to close, and shake to mix thoroughly. Add the chicken pieces and shake to coat.

Spray a nonstick skillet lightly with nonstick vegetable oil, add the sunflower oil, and place over medium heat. When the oil is hot add the coated chicken and brown lightly. Remove the chicken to a heavy 3- or 4-quart saucepan and set aside.

Add the onions, garlic, and pepper to the skillet and sauté gently until soft, stirring occasionally. Add the tomatoes, chickpeas, and ¾ cup of the reserved tomato liquid. Bring to a boil and cook 5 minutes.

Pour the vegetables over the chicken, cover, and place over low-medium heat. Simmer 30 minutes or until the chicken is tender. Do not overcook. It may be necessary to add a bit of tomato liquid while the chicken is simmering.

To finish, stir in the sherry and olives and cook over moderate-high heat 2 minutes longer. Taste, correct seasoning, and serve immediately.

*Yield: 6 diet servings*
*Calories per serving: 272*

---

### CHICKPEAS JEREZ MENU PLAN

*898 Calories (plus 200-calorie snack)*

Coffee, tea, or noncaloric beverages as desired

### BREAKFAST

½ cup fresh or unsweetened frozen blueberries
½ cup plain low-fat yogurt
1 frozen waffle, heated

(*Substitute:* Basic Breakfast 3)

### LUNCH

Swiss Turkey
  2 slices whole wheat bread
  1 ounce Swiss cheese
  1 ounce turkey
  Lettuce
  ½ tomato, sliced
1 carrot

(*Substitute:* Basic Lunch 1)

### DINNER

1 diet serving Chickpeas Jerez
½ serving Basic Super Salad
1 cup cooked broccoli
1 cup skim milk

## *Chicken–Lima Bean Soufflé*

Although this recipe makes six diet servings, it is perfect for a family of four with only one dieter.

It's extremely simple to prepare and looks elegant and fussed over.

> 1 can condensed cream of mushroom soup
> ⅓ cup low-fat milk
> 1½ cups diced frozen (thawed) or cooked leftover chicken
> 1½ packages frozen baby lima beans, cooked and drained completely
> ¼ teaspoon dried oregano or 1 teaspoon fresh
> 3 eggs, separated
> 2 ounces cheddar cheese, shredded

Place the soup in a bowl and mix with the milk to thin slightly. Add the chicken, beans, and oregano. Turn into an attractive shallow baking dish or casserole. Bake 10 minutes in a preheated 375°F oven.

While the chicken is heating, beat the egg yolks until foamy. Fold in the cheese.

Beat the egg whites until stiff but not dry. Fold into the yolks. Pile the eggs over the hot chicken and return to the oven. Bake an additional 30 minutes or until puffy and brown.

Serve immediately.

> *Yield: 6 diet servings*
> *Calories per serving: 292*

≈§ *Cut your food into very small pieces to slow your eating. Except spaghetti. Keep it as long as possible so it keeps falling off the fork.*

## CHICKEN–LIMA BEAN SOUFFLÉ
## MENU PLAN

*885 Calories (plus 200-calorie snack)*

Coffee, tea, or noncaloric beverages as desired

### BREAKFAST

Fruit Cup
  ½ cup fresh or unsweetened frozen straw-
    berries
  ½ cup cut-up cantaloupe
  1 teaspoon wheat germ
  1 cup plain low-fat yogurt

(*Substitute:* Basic Breakfast 1)

### LUNCH

Turkey Salad
  2 ounces turkey
  1 small tomato, chopped
  1 cucumber, chopped
  1 scallion, chopped
  Mustard *or* 1 teaspoon diet mayonnaise
  1 1-ounce whole wheat bread pocket
  1 cup skim milk

(*Substitute:* Basic Lunch 3)

### DINNER

  1 diet serving Chicken–Lima Bean Soufflé
  ⅔ cup cooked carrots
  ½ serving Basic Super Salad

## Savory Bean Soup

The very delicate flavor of Italian beans is somewhat diminished by the original freezing process so we do not recommend freezing this soup. You may, of course, prepare it early and reheat it slowly at serving time.

4 packages frozen Italian beans
1 cup cold water
½ teaspoon coarse salt
½ teaspoon dried savory *or* 1 sprig fresh
6 ounces chicken breast (after boning, skinning, and removing all visible fat)
5 cubes chicken bouillon, dissolved in 4 cups boiling water
Pinch nutmeg
Salt and freshly ground pepper to taste

Combine the beans, water, salt, and savory in a saucepan for which you have a cover. Cook according to the directions on the package. Purée the beans in their cooking liquid and set aside.

Poach the chicken breast in a small nonstick skillet in just enough bouillon to half cover. When one side of the breast is opaque, turn and poach the other side. Be careful not to overcook the chicken. Using a slotted spoon, remove the breast to a small plate and set aside.

Combine the poaching liquid, the remaining bouillon, and the bean purée in a 2-quart saucepan or stockpot. Add the nutmeg and reheat.

Meanwhile, shred the chicken breast or slice it into thin julienne strips.

When the soup is reheated, taste and add salt and pepper.

Ladle into individual bowls and garnish with equal amounts of chicken.

*Yield: 4 diet servings*
*Calories per serving: 165*

## *SAVORY BEAN SOUP MENU PLAN*

*900 Calories (plus 200-calorie snack)*

**Coffee, tea, or noncaloric beverages as desired**

### BREAKFAST

1 bagel, toasted
¼ cup low-fat cottage cheese

(*Substitute:* Basic Breakfast 3)

### LUNCH

Warm Cold Cuts
4 ounces lean cold cuts, fried in nonstick pan
½ serving Basic Super Salad
1 tablespoon diet mayonnaise mixed with
    strong mustard
1 1-ounce whole wheat bread pocket
½ dill pickle
½ cup skim milk

(*Substitute:* Basic Lunch 1)

### DINNER

1 diet serving Savory Bean Soup
½ serving Basic Super Salad
1 hard roll
1 cup skim milk

## Double-Bean Salad

This salad must be allowed to chill at least 4 hours. You may prepare it a day early and refrigerate it overnight. Be certain it is well covered while chilling.

1 package frozen French-style green beans
1 package frozen baby lima beans
1 medium red onion, finely chopped
½ cup chopped parsley
1 tablespoon olive oil
3 tablespoons Sherry Vinegar (page 23)
1½ packages Equal (low-calorie sweetener)
⅛ teaspoon dry mustard
⅛ teaspoon paprika
½ teaspoon dried basil
½ teaspoon dried oregano
⅛ teaspoon garlic powder
Salt and freshly ground black pepper to taste
2 canned pimientos, chopped
6 ounces smoked turkey, shredded

Cook the green beans and lima beans separately. Drain, cool, and mix together in a bowl. Add the onion and parsley and toss to mix.

Combine the oil, vinegar, Equal, mustard, paprika, basil, oregano, garlic powder, salt, and pepper in a small bowl. Whisk until blended. Correct seasoning. Pour over the vegetables and toss. Refrigerate at least 4 hours, tossing 2 or 3 times to keep dressing from settling on the bottom.

Garnish with pimientos and turkey.

*Yield: 4 diet servings*
*Calories per serving: 256*

## DOUBLE-BEAN SALAD MENU PLAN
*896 Calories (plus 200-calorie snack)*

Coffee, tea, or noncaloric beverages as desired

### BREAKFAST
1 egg, any style (use nonstick skillet to fry or scramble)
1 frozen waffle
1 tablespoon diet margarine
1 tablespoon diet maple syrup

(*Substitute:* Basic Breakfast 2)


### LUNCH
Cheese Tacos
2 taco shells
2 ounces Lite-line cheese
1 tomato, chopped
½ small onion, chopped
1 cup alfalfa sprouts
Salsa to taste
1 cup skim milk

(*Substitute:* Basic Lunch 3)


### DINNER
1 diet serving Double-Bean Salad
½ cup unsweetened pineapple chunks
1 cup skim milk

## *Russian Vegetable Salad*

Vegetarians love this unique salad, but even meat eaters will find it satisfying.

Prepare this dish early in the day if you like, but keep it in a cool (not cold) place. This salad should be served at room temperature to bring out the natural flavors of all the ingredients.

> 1 package frozen peas
> Pinch baking soda
> 2 apples, peeled, cored, and diced
> 1 tablespoon freshly squeezed lemon juice
> 4 large new potatoes (1 pound), peeled, boiled, diced, and cooled
> 2 sour pickles, coarsely minced
> 1 medium onion, diced
> 2 medium cucumbers, peeled, seeded, and diced
> 2 cups canned white kidney beans, drained
> 3 tablespoons Sour Half-and-Half (page 28)
> 3 tablespoons diet mayonnaise
> 1 teaspoon vinegar, preferably tarragon
> Salt to taste

Cook the peas according to the directions on the package, substituting baking soda for salt, until just tender. Drain and immediately immerse in cold water for 3 minutes to halt the cooking process and retain the brilliant color. Drain thoroughly.

Combine the apples and lemon juice. Toss.

Combine the peas, apples, potatoes, pickles, onion, cucumbers, and beans in a large bowl.

Blend the half-and-half, mayonnaise, vinegar, and salt.

Add the sauce to the vegetables and toss. Let stand at room temperature a few minutes before serving.

> *Yield: 6 diet servings*
> *Calories per serving: 262*

## RUSSIAN VEGETABLE SALAD MENU PLAN

*888 Calories (plus 200-calorie snack)*

Coffee, tea, or noncaloric beverages as desired

### BREAKFAST

½ bagel, toasted
1 teaspoon peanut butter
1 teaspoon diet jelly
1 cup skim milk

(*Substitute:* Basic Breakfast 1)

### LUNCH

Tuna Salad
　3½ ounces water-packed tuna
　½ cucumber, chopped
　½ green pepper, chopped
　1 scallion, chopped
　1 tablespoon diet mayonnaise
　1 1-ounce whole wheat bread pocket
　½ cup skim milk

(*Substitute:* Basic Lunch 1)

### DINNER

1 diet serving Russian Vegetable Salad
½ serving Super Coleslaw
1 small orange
1 rice cake
½ cup skim milk

## *Cheddar Cheese Pudding*

Save this unusual dish for an evening when you have time to prepare it just before serving.

> 1 chicken bouillon cube, in ½ cup boiling water
> 2 packages frozen baby peas
> 1 pound carrots, scraped and grated
> 2 inner stalks celery with leaves, chopped
> 2 onions, finely chopped
> 2 tablespoons chopped parsley
> ¼ teaspoon salt
> ⅛ teaspoon freshly ground pepper
> ⅛ teaspoon celery salt
> Nonstick vegetable oil spray
> 2 tablespoons whipped butter *or* diet margarine
> 3 tablespoons whole wheat flour
> ⅔ cup low-fat milk
> 3 medium eggs, beaten
> 3½ ounces cheddar cheese, grated

Bring the bouillon to a boil in a medium saucepan; add the peas and cook according to the package directions. Drain and reserve the cooking liquid and the peas separately.

Measure ½ cup plus 2 tablespoons cooking liquid (if there isn't enough, add water to get the required amount). Return the liquid to the saucepan and add the carrots, celery, and onions. Bring to a rapid boil, reduce heat, and cover. Cook 15 minutes or until the vegetables are very tender. Drain and reserve the liquid.

Add the parsley, salt, pepper, and celery salt to the vegetables. Turn into a blender jar and purée. Add some cooking liquid if necessary to get a smooth blend.

Spray the bottom and sides of a baking dish or casserole with nonstick vegetable oil. Pour in the vegetable purée and smooth. Arrange the peas over the purée and set aside.

Melt the butter in a small saucepan. Stir in the flour and cook 30 seconds. Stirring continually, add the milk and blend well. Simmer 2 minutes longer, then remove from the heat.

Whisk in the eggs, beating continually, then the cheese. Correct seasoning and pour over the vegetables.

Bake in a preheated 350 °F oven 45 minutes or until a cake tester comes out clean.

*Yield: 6 diet servings*
*Calories per serving: 253*

---

### CHEDDAR CHEESE PUDDING MENU PLAN

*894 Calories (plus 200-calorie snack)*

Coffee, tea, or noncaloric beverages as desired

#### BREAKFAST

1 egg, scrambled with
1 teaspoon butter, topped with
¼ cup low-fat cottage cheese
1 teaspoon diet jelly
1 slice whole wheat toast

(*Substitute:* Basic Breakfast 2)

#### LUNCH

Pepper Steak
4 ounces lean beef cold cuts, warmed
1 green pepper and 1 small onion, chopped
and sautéed in 1 tablespoon oil
1 tomato, chopped
Basil and oregano to taste
1 1-ounce whole wheat bread pocket
½ cup skim milk

(*Substitute:* Basic Lunch 1)

#### DINNER

1 diet serving Cheddar Cheese Pudding
½ serving Super Coleslaw
1 cup skim milk

## *Kansas City Fish Chowder*

You can enjoy this unusual fish soup less than 20 minutes after
you start it. Refrigerate cooled leftovers and eat them the
next day.

> 3 chicken bouillon cubes, dissolved in 2 cups boiling
>     water
> 3 packages frozen peas
> ½ head Boston or other lettuce, washed and shred-
>     ded
> ½ teaspoon dried savory or 1 teaspoon fresh,
>     chopped
> 2 scallions, white and green parts, trimmed and
>     finely chopped
> 1 tablespoon whipped butter *or* diet margarine
> 3 cups low-fat milk
> 1 7-ounce can water-packed white tuna, drained
>     and flaked
> Salt and pepper to taste
> 2 tablespoons chopped pimientos

Bring 1 cup bouillon to a rapid boil in a 3-quart saucepan.
Add the peas, lettuce, and savory. Bring back to a boil, cover,
reduce the heat, and cook 5 minutes or until the peas are soft
but still bright green. Remove from the heat and stir in the
scallions and butter.

Transfer two thirds of the vegetables and ½ cup of their
liquid to a blender or food processor and purée. Return the
purée to the saucepan with the reserved liquid and stir.

Combine the remaining bouillon with the milk in a small
saucepan and bring it just to the boiling point. Remove from
the heat and stir into the purée, mixing thoroughly.

Add the tuna and heat 2 minutes. Correct seasoning with
salt and pepper.

Garnish each serving with 1 teaspoon pimientos.

*Yield: 6 diet servings*
*Calories per serving: 221*

## KANSAS CITY FISH CHOWDER MENU PLAN
*895 Calories (plus 200-calorie snack)*

Coffee, tea, or noncaloric beverages as desired

### BREAKFAST

1 cup tomato juice
1 slice whole wheat toast
1 slice Swiss cheese

(*Substitute:* Basic Breakfast 3)

### LUNCH

Fruit Dip
1 cup plain low-fat yogurt
½ cup fresh or unsweetened frozen strawberries, cut in half
½ cantaloupe, cut into sticks
3 rice cakes

(*Substitute:* Basic Lunch 2)

### DINNER

1 diet serving Kansas City Fish Chowder
1 serving Super Spinach Salad
1 cup skim milk

&§ *Hate to exercise in public? Try pulling down the shades, putting on some fifties dance music, and moving down memory lane.*

## Bean-and-Parsley Salad

Prepare this salad at least 24 hours ahead. It's yummy!

> 2 cups pea beans, soaked in water to cover over-
>   night
> ½ teaspoon baking soda
> ⅔ cup wine vinegar
> 1 tablespoon olive oil
> ½ cup finely chopped flat leaf or curly parsley
> 1 clove garlic, finely minced
> Salt and freshly ground pepper to taste

Drain the beans and place them in a 3-quart saucepan. Add enough water to cover to about 2 inches above the beans. Stir in the baking soda and bring to a boil. Skim off the foam, reduce the heat, and simmer until the beans are soft but not mushy. (Depending on the age of the beans, the time may vary somewhere between 45 minutes and 1½ hours.) Drain thoroughly.

Transfer the beans to a bowl and sprinkle with a third of the vinegar. Toss gently to allow the vinegar to be absorbed. Repeat this process with the second and final thirds. Taste between additions to determine whether the beans are tart enough for your taste.

Sprinkle the oil, parsley, and garlic over the beans and toss again, lightly. Season with salt and pepper.

Marinate in the refrigerator at least 24 hours. If necessary, correct seasoning before serving.

*Yield: 6 diet servings*
*Calories per serving: 256*

## BEAN-AND-PARSLEY SALAD MENU PLAN

*909 Calories (plus 200-calorie snack)*

Coffee, tea, or noncaloric beverages as desired

### BREAKFAST

1 corn muffin
¼ cup low-fat cottage cheese
1 tablespoon diet jelly

(*Substitute:* Basic Breakfast 3)

### LUNCH

3 ounces chicken
1 serving Super Spinach Salad, chopped
1 1-ounce whole wheat bread pocket
½ cup skim milk

(*Substitute:* Basic Lunch 1)

### DINNER

1 diet serving Bean-and-Parsley Salad
1 cup fresh or unsweetened frozen strawberries
   *or* 1 orange
1 cup skim milk

꒛ *When you eat away from home, wear clothes that are a little too tight. Clothes that refuse to expand cause the number of calories you consume to shrink.*

## Soul Food Salad

Dishes like black-eyed peas and rice with red gravy, greens, chitlins have long been central to black cuisine but were practically unknown elsewhere. So when food lovers were introduced to soul food in the 1960s, they took to it like gluttons to *foie gras*. Our version removes almost all the fat.

When chilled in the refrigerator overnight, it's even better.

> 1 slice lean bacon, chopped
> 2 cloves garlic, bruised
> 1½ cups black-eyed peas
> ½ teaspoon baking soda
> 1 bay leaf
> ¼ cup cider vinegar
> 2 tablespoons freshly squeezed lemon juice
> 1 tablespoon vegetable oil
> ½ teaspoon salt
> ⅛ teaspoon freshly ground black pepper
> 12 ounces spinach, stems removed, washed
>     thoroughly, and dried
> 2 medium tomatoes, peeled, seeded, and chopped
> Salt and pepper to taste

Sauté the bacon until just brown in a 3-quart heavy-bottomed saucepan. Add the garlic and sauté, stirring, 15 seconds. Remove the pan from the heat. Combine the peas, baking soda, and bay leaf and add to the saucepan. Add enough water to cover to 1 inch above the peas; stir and bring to a boil. Skim off any foam that forms, reduce the heat, and simmer about 30 minutes. Skim the foam during the cooking process.

When the peas are sufficiently tender, but not mushy, drain thoroughly. Discard the bay leaf.

Carefully remove the garlic to a small bowl and mash it with a fork. Add the vinegar and mix thoroughly. Set aside.

Transfer the peas to a mixing bowl and slowly sprinkle with the seasoned vinegar. Toss the peas between sprinklings, to allow them to absorb the vinegar. There should be no liquid in the bottom of the bowl. Add the lemon juice the same way, tossing between additions. Sprinkle the peas with the oil, salt, and pepper. Toss lightly. Refrigerate at least 2 hours.

Just before serving, pat the spinach leaves dry and chop them. Toss with the tomatoes and add to the marinated peas. Toss again, taste, and correct seasoning.

*Yield: 6 diet servings*
*Calories per serving: 236*

---

## SOUL FOOD SALAD MENU PLAN

*901 Calories (plus 200-calorie snack)*

**Coffee, tea, or noncaloric beverages as desired**

### BREAKFAST

1 egg, any style (use nonstick pan)
1 English muffin

(*Substitute:* Basic Breakfast 2)

### LUNCH

Crunchy Pocket
2 ounces turkey *or* chicken
½ cup red cabbage
1 dill pickle, chopped
1 tablespoon diet mayonnaise
1 1-ounce whole wheat bread pocket
1 cup skim milk

(*Substitute:* Basic Lunch 3)

### DINNER

1 diet serving Soul Food Salad
2 ounces French bread
1 cup skim milk

# 10

## Fast Meals

### Ravioli Reward

This dish takes only as long to prepare as it takes to cook the ravioli. An easy, satisfying dinner for one.

> 2 cubes chicken bouillon, dissolved in 4 cups
>    boiling water
> 7 ounces frozen cheese ravioli
> 1 small can stewed tomatoes
> 1 teaspoon cornstarch
> ⅛ teaspoon dried oregano
> ¼ teaspoon garlic salt
> 1 teaspoon green pepper flakes
> 1 teaspoon lemon juice
> Salt and pepper to taste
> ½ ounce Parmesan cheese, grated

Bring the bouillon to a boil. Add the ravioli and cook according to the package directions.

Meanwhile, combine the tomatoes and cornstarch in a small saucepan and mix well. Place the saucepan over moderate heat and cook until the tomatoes begin to thicken. Add the oregano, garlic salt, pepper flakes, lemon juice, salt and pepper. Stir and cook 1 minute longer. Correct seasoning and pour over the drained ravioli. Sprinkle with cheese and serve.

*Yield: 1 diet serving*
*Calories per serving: 374*

## RAVIOLI REWARD MENU PLAN

*905 Calories (plus 200-calorie snack)*

Coffee, tea, or noncaloric beverages as desired

## BREAKFAST

1 cup plain low-fat yogurt
¾ cup fresh or unsweetened frozen strawberries
1 tablespoon wheat germ

(*Substitute:* Basic Breakfast 1)

## LUNCH

Chicken in the Grass
    2 preformed taco shells
    2½ ounces chicken, shredded
    1 cup loosely packed alfalfa sprouts
    1 tomato, chopped
    1 scallion, chopped (optional)
    1 teaspoon diet salad dressing
    Salsa to taste
1 cup skim milk

(*Substitute:* Basic Lunch 1)

## DINNER

1 diet serving Ravioli Reward
1 cup cooked broccoli
1 small banana

## *Quick Curry Noodles*

The fastest chicken-and-noodle curry in the West.

    4 ounces Superoni fettuccine
    4 ounces canned Swanson's Chicken à la King
    1 small can stewed tomatoes
    1 tablespoon curry powder (or less to taste)
    ½ teaspoon garlic powder
    ½ teaspoon sugar

Cook the fettuccine, drain, and reserve.

Combine the chicken and tomatoes in a saucepan. Stir in the curry, garlic, and sugar. Taste and correct seasoning. Heat thoroughly, pour over the pasta, and toss.

    *Yield: 2 diet servings*
    *Calories per serving: 287*

◄§ *Can't seem to end the meal? Leave the table and go somewhere in the house away from the food. Busy yourself with a chore or indulge yourself by reading a good book or calling a friend. In an hour, you will feel full and be able to clear up the table without nibbling.*

◄§ *Never, never stand next to a buffet table or bowl of peanuts or chips at a party. Find a friendly plant instead.*

## *QUICK CURRY NOODLES MENU PLAN*

*910 Calories (plus 200-calorie snack)*

Coffee, tea, or noncaloric beverages as desired

### BREAKFAST

1 small orange
1 1-ounce whole wheat bread pocket, toasted
1 teaspoon diet jelly
1 cup skim milk

(*Substitute:* Basic Breakfast 1)

### LUNCH

Cheeseburger Taco
   2 taco shells
   2 ounces chopped lean meat, broiled, or
      fried in nonstick pan
   1 ounce cheddar cheese, shredded
   ½ small tomato, chopped
   Lettuce
1 cup skim milk

(*Substitute:* Basic Lunch 1)

### DINNER

1 diet serving Quick Curry Noodles
1 serving any Super Salad
½ cup skim milk

## *Noodles for One*

This delicious blend of flavors is quicker than quick. And only one pot to wash.

> 2 ounces broad egg noodles
> ¼ cup low-fat cottage cheese
> ½ tablespoon chopped parsley
> ½ tablespoon chopped dill
> Salt and pepper to taste

Cook the noodles in a medium-sized saucepan. Drain thoroughly, return to the pot, and add the cheese, parsley, and dill. Toss, taste, and add salt and pepper.

> *Yield: 1 diet serving*
> *Calories per serving: 265*

✎§ *Not losing weight fast enough?*
*Spend more time exercising.*

✎§ *Do your fingers keep walking toward*
*your mouth, carrying nibbling food?*
*Try nibbling on Grape-nuts or a*
*Swiss cereal called Muesli. Eat it*
*only with your fingers. You'll spend*
*as much time picking up the*
*dropped cereal as actually eating it.*

✎§ *Do your spouse or children eat your*
*snacks? Conceal them in a container*
*marked "liver."*

## NOODLES FOR ONE MENU PLAN

*901 Calories (plus 200-calorie snack)*

Coffee, tea, or noncaloric beverages as desired

### BREAKFAST

1 cup vanilla-flavored low-fat yogurt
1 tablespoon wheat germ

(*Substitute:* Basic Breakfast 1)

### LUNCH

Tuna Sandwich
2 slices whole wheat toast
3½ ounces water-packed tuna, mixed with
½ cucumber, chopped
1 teaspoon fresh dill *or* ½ teaspoon dried
Lemon juice
1 tablespoon diet mayonnaise
½ cup skim milk

(*Substitute:* Basic Lunch 1)

### DINNER

1 diet serving Noodles for One
1 serving Super Spinach Salad
½ cup skim milk

## *Hurry-Up Curry-Up*

An easy and satisfying dinner for two dieters.

    1 cup cooked rice
    1 4-ounce can boned turkey chunks
    1 small can mushrooms
    1 small can stewed tomatoes
    1 teaspoon cornstarch
    1 tablespoon curry powder (or less to taste)
    ½ teaspoon garlic powder

Heat the rice in a vegetable steamer and keep warm. Combine the turkey, mushrooms, and tomatoes in a small saucepan. Sprinkle with cornstarch and mix thoroughly. Sprinkle in the curry and garlic and stir. Heat, stirring, until the sauce thickens.

Serve over steamed rice.

*Yield: 2 diet servings*
*Calories per serving: 224*


*Don't worry if the meal you order in
a restaurant comes with bread
crumbs, sauce, or butter. Remove as
much as you can and enjoy the
meal. Those few extra calories will
not ruin your diet.*


*Is your exercycle a home for spiders?
Get yourself a small radio or tape
player with earphones and start ped-
aling. The spiders will go elsewhere.*

## *HURRY-UP CURRY-UP MENU PLAN*

*888 Calories (plus 200-calorie snack)*

Coffee, tea, or noncaloric beverages as desired

### BREAKFAST

½ cup fresh or unsweetened frozen blueberries
*or* ½ grapefruit
1 frozen waffle *or* 1 frozen pancake, heated
½ cup low-fat cottage cheese

(*Substitute:* Basic Breakfast 4)

### LUNCH

2 preformed taco shells
4 ounces lean cold cuts, shredded
1 ounce Lite-line cheese, shredded
½ cup shredded lettuce
Salsa and onions to taste
½ cup skim milk

(*Substitute:* Basic Lunch 1)

### DINNER

1 diet serving Hurry-Up Curry-Up
1 serving Super Coleslaw

## *Chicken Gauguin*

Easy, easy, easy! Fast, fast, fast. Yum, yum, yummy! Prepare it ahead and refrigerate it if you wish, but don't freeze this dish unless you have used leftover home-cooked chicken.

½ cup canned crushed pineapple in juice
2 tablespoons honey
2 tablespoons prepared mustard
1 tablespoon toasted sesame seeds
6 ounces frozen (thawed) cooked or home-cooked (skinless) chicken, diced
1 cup cooked rice, reheated or kept warm
1 scallion, white and green parts, trimmed and minced
1 tablespoon chopped pimiento

Spread the pineapple on the bottom of an 8-inch nonstick skillet. Set aside.

Combine the honey, mustard, and sesame in a small bowl and mix well. Add the chicken and mix to coat. Turn the seasoned chicken into the skillet and spread gently over the pineapple. Cook, covered, over moderate heat, 10 minutes or until heated through. Shake the pan occasionally during the cooking process.

Meanwhile, transfer the heated rice to a serving bowl and add the scallion. Toss and keep warm.

Serve the chicken over the rice and garnish with pimiento.

*Yield: 2 diet servings*
*Calories per serving: 324*

> ⋵§ *Some of us eat fast so we don't notice what we're eating. But our bodies notice.*

## *CHICKEN GAUGUIN MENU PLAN*

*891 Calories (plus 200-calorie snack)*

Coffee, tea, or noncaloric beverages as desired

### BREAKFAST

1 frozen cheese blintz, cooked in a nonstick
skillet and served with
½ cup artificially sweetened low-fat yogurt
1 cup fresh or unsweetened frozen strawberries
*or* ½ cup sliced bananas

(*Substitute:* Basic Breakfast 1)

### LUNCH

Tuna Pocket
  3½ ounces water-packed tuna, drained
  ½ cucumber, chopped
  ½ green pepper, chopped
  1 scallion, chopped
  1 tablespoon diet mayonnaise
  1 1-ounce whole wheat bread pocket
½ cup skim milk

(*Substitute:* Basic Lunch 1)

### DINNER

1 diet serving Chicken Gauguin
½ serving any Super Salad
½ cup skim milk

## *Egg Cups Florentine*

A recipe that's easy to divide — or multiply. It's particularly suitable for one person because it's fast and uses foods you are likely to have in your refrigerator.

>    4 large tomatoes, peeled
>    Salt
>    2 cups cooked rice, reheated in steamer
>    2 packages chopped frozen spinach, cooked and
>       drained
>    1 teaspoon garlic salt
>    2 scallions, trimmed and finely chopped
>    1 ounce Parmesan cheese, grated
>    4 eggs

Slice off the top of each tomato and carefully scoop out the seeds and centers. Do not break through either the bottoms or walls of the tomatoes. Sprinkle the insides with salt and turn upside down on 3 layers of paper towels to drain. Discard the tomato seeds and chop the pulp.

Combine the rice, spinach, garlic salt, scallions, and tomato pulp and mix well.

Arrange a bed of rice mix on an attractive, ovenproof serving platter. Sprinkle with half the cheese. Arrange the tomatoes on the rice mix (open side up) and crack one egg into each.

Place the platter in a preheated 400°F oven for 7 minutes or until the whites begin to set. Sprinkle with the remaining cheese. Return to the oven and bake until the cheese begins to brown and the egg whites are completely set. Do not overcook.

Serve immediately.

>    *Yield: 4 diet servings*
>    *Calories per serving: 261*

# EGG CUPS FLORENTINE MENU PLAN

*892 Calories (plus 200-calorie snack)*

Coffee, tea, or noncaloric beverages as desired

## BREAKFAST

1 small orange
½ English muffin, toasted
1 teaspoon diet jelly
1 cup skim milk

(*Substitute:* Basic Breakfast 4)

## LUNCH

Ham and Cheese Taco
    2 preformed taco shells
    2 ounces (2 slices) lean ham, chopped
    1 slice Lite-line cheese, shredded
    Shredded lettuce
    Salsa to taste
    1 cup skim milk

(*Substitute:* Basic Lunch 3)

## DINNER

1 diet serving Egg Cups Florentine
1 serving any Super Salad
1 cup fresh or unsweetened frozen strawberries

## Peking Pork

This dish uses leftovers nicely. It may also be divided in half easily to make a quick dinner for one.

> 2 teaspoons vegetable oil
> 2 eggs, beaten
> 4 ounces boiled ham, sliced and cut into thin strips
> 1 scallion, slivered
> ¼ cup shredded Chinese or savoy cabbage
> 1 tablespoon chicken broth
> 2 teaspoons soy sauce
> 1 tablespoon sherry
> ¼ teaspoon dried ginger (more if you like)
> ¼ teaspoon sugar
> 1 cup cooked white rice

Brush a nonstick skillet with the oil and heat. Add the eggs and scramble them until they are the consistency you like. Remove to a warm plate.

Add the ham, scallion, and cabbage and stir-fry 1 minute. Remove from the heat.

Quickly combine the broth, soy sauce, sherry, ginger, and sugar. Stir and add to the skillet.

Return the skillet to the heat and stir-fry 1 minute longer. Combine with the eggs and toss.

Serve over the cooked rice.

> *Yield: 2 diet servings*
> *Calories per serving: 334*

◄§ *Feel you must serve dessert to your guests? Buy (don't bake) individual goodies like small tarts, little cakes, or puff pastries. Buy only enough for your guests. This prevents leftovers and temptation.*

## *PEKING PORK MENU PLAN*

*885 Calories (plus 200-calorie snack)*

Coffee, tea, or noncaloric beverages as desired

## BREAKFAST

½ cup unsweetened pineapple chunks
½ cup low-fat cottage cheese
1 slice raisin bread toast

(*Substitute:* Basic Breakfast 1)

## LUNCH

Green and Red Tuna
    1 large green pepper, filled with
    2 ounces water-packed tuna
    ½ tomato, chopped
    1 tablespoon diet mayonnaise
    1 scallion (optional)
1 1-ounce whole wheat bread pocket
1 cup skim milk

(*Substitute:* Basic Lunch 3)

## DINNER

1 diet serving Peking Pork
½ serving Super Spinach Salad
½ cup skim milk

## *Klosters Cheese Bits*

This very quick and simple dish is a favorite of jet-set skiers who frequent the Swiss resort of Klosters. It's a perfect meal for cold evenings or after winter sports. Come to think of it, it's delicious any time.

> Nonstick vegetable oil spray
> 2 packages frozen chopped spinach, cooked and
>     drained thoroughly
> 2 scallions, green tops only, minced
> ½ pound potatoes, peeled, cooked and mashed with
>     ¼ cup buttermilk
> 1 teaspoon garlic salt
> 2 thin slices (2 ounces) smoked ham, all fat trimmed
>     and cut in half
> 4 eggs
> 2 ounces Gruyère *or* Swiss cheese, grated
> Nutmeg to taste

Spray 4 individual shallow casserole dishes with nonstick vegetable oil and set aside.

Combine the drained spinach, scallions, potatoes, and garlic salt in a small bowl. Mix thoroughly and gently press a quarter of this mix into each casserole. Smooth the top with a spatula.

Place a half slice of ham in the center of each dish, crack an egg over the ham, and bake in a preheated 400°F oven 7 minutes or until the whites begin to set.

Remove from the oven and sprinkle each dish with a quarter of the cheese. Return the casseroles to the oven and bake an additional 2 to 3 minutes or until the cheese has melted.

Sprinkle with a little nutmeg and serve immediately.

> *Yield: 4 diet servings*
> *Calories per serving: 235*

## KLOSTERS CHEESE BITS MENU PLAN

*894 Calories (plus 200-calorie snack)*

Coffee, tea, or noncaloric beverages as desired

### BREAKFAST

1 small orange, sliced
1 medium egg, scrambled or fried in nonstick
   pan
1 slice whole wheat toast
1 tablespoon diet jelly

(*Substitute:* Basic Breakfast 2)

### LUNCH

½ cup low-fat cottage cheese, flavored with
1 teaspoon Bran-and-Spice Sprinkle *or* Cottage
   Cheese Sprinkle (page 29)
1 corn muffin
1 small banana

(*Substitute:* Basic Lunch 3)

### DINNER

1 diet serving Klosters Cheese Bits
1 serving Basic Super Salad
1 cup skim milk

᪣ *Don't order tuna or egg salad when
you eat out. The mayonnaise content is too high for your diet.*

## *Chicken Toledo*

One serving may be refrigerated and reheated or eaten cold the next day.

> 1 teaspoon sunflower *or* safflower oil
> 1 small clove garlic, minced
> 1 small can chickpeas, drained
> 1 small can stewed tomatoes
> ½ cup frozen chopped bell peppers
> 6 ounces frozen diced cooked chicken
> Pinch ground cumin
> ¼ teaspoon chili powder
> Salt and pepper to taste
> 3 tablespoons whiskey
> Chopped parsley for garnish

Heat the oil and garlic together in a medium-sized nonstick skillet. Add the chickpeas, tomatoes, peppers, chicken, cumin, chili, and salt and pepper. Increase the heat and cook, stirring occasionally, until the liquid has almost cooked out. Add the whiskey and cook another 3 minutes.

Garnish with parsley.

> *Yield: 2 diet servings*
> *Calories per serving: 331*

&#x25c4;&sect; *The snack is such a good part of the diet, so enjoy it! It isn't medicine to be taken in one swallow.*

&#x25c4;&sect; *If you're hungry, eat your salad while you prepare supper. That way you'll be nibbling on something you should be eating.*

## *CHICKEN TOLEDO MENU PLAN*

*899 Calories (plus 200-calorie snack)*

Coffee, tea, or noncaloric beverages as desired

### BREAKFAST

½ cup fresh or unsweetened frozen blueberries
*or* ½ small banana
1 teaspoon sugar
½ cup plain low-fat yogurt
1 frozen waffle, heated

(*Substitute:* Basic Breakfast 3)

### LUNCH

Pepper Steak
4 ounces lean beef cold cuts, heated in nonstick pan
1 green pepper and 1 small onion, chopped
and sautéed in
1 teaspoon oil, sprinkled with
Oregano and basil
1 tomato
1 1-ounce whole wheat bread pocket
½ cup skim milk

(*Substitute:* Basic Lunch 1)

### DINNER

1 diet serving  Chicken Toledo
½ serving any Super Salad
1 orange
1 cup skim milk

## *Express Lentil Stew*

This stew is fast and easy to prepare and may be eaten immediately after cooking, but you will reap real gustatory rewards if you throw it together the night before and let the flavors blend overnight in the refrigerator.

Unless you use previously frozen chicken, you may freeze this stew in individual-serving containers, and a truly delicious meal will be only as far away as your freezer.

In either case, reheat the chicken and lentils slowly before serving.

> 6 fresh chicken thighs (18 ounces), skinned and all
>     visible fat removed
> 1 can Progresso (or other) Lentil Soup
> 2 small cloves garlic
> ½ teaspoon coarse salt
> ⅛ teaspoon mace
> 1 small bay leaf

Brown the chicken on both sides over moderate heat in a nonstick skillet that will hold all the thighs in one layer.

Drain the soup, reserving the lentils and stock separately. When the chicken is brown, force the garlic through a press over the chicken. Add the lentils, salt, mace, bay leaf, and ¼ cup of the soup stock and mix. Cover, reduce the heat, and simmer 15 minutes or until the meat is tender.

Remove the bay leaf before serving.

> *Yield: 4 diet servings*
> *Calories per serving: 191*

 

**◄§ Do you take an elevator rather than stairs because you're in a hurry? If you're in a hurry to lose weight, choose the stairs.**

## *EXPRESS LENTIL STEW MENU PLAN*

*910 Calories (plus 200-calorie snack)*

Coffee, tea, or noncaloric beverages as desired

## BREAKFAST

½ grapefruit
1 slice rye toast, topped with
1 slice Swiss cheese, melted

(*Substitute:* Basic Breakfast 3)

## LUNCH

Hearty Salad
1 hard-boiled egg, chopped
2 ounces lean cold cuts, chopped
1 dill pickle, chopped
1 tablespoon diet mayonnaise mixed with
mustard
1 carrot
2 rice cakes
½ cup skim milk

(*Substitute:* Basic Lunch 1)

## DINNER

1 diet serving Express Lentil Stew
1 cup cooked broccoli
1 serving Basic Super Salad
1 cup skim milk

## Oysters Rock-a-Bye

This simple dish is a quickie version of the old gourmet standby Oysters Rockefeller. Try it. You'll feel like a million.

12 fresh oysters, shucked, with their liquid
4 tablespoons dry white wine
1 teaspoon Sherry Vinegar (page 23)
½ cup cooked fresh or frozen chopped spinach, drained thoroughly
1 English muffin, split and toasted
⅓ cup condensed cream of chicken soup
1 teaspoon prepared mustard
Paprika

Combine the oyster liquid, wine, and vinegar in a small non-stick skillet. Bring to a boil, reduce the heat, and add the oysters in one layer. Cook only until the edges of the oysters begin to curl. Remove the oysters with a slotted spoon and reserve their liquid.

Arrange half the spinach on one half muffin and top with 6 oysters. Repeat on second half muffin. Place on a nonstick baking sheet and set aside.

Combine the soup, mustard, and 4 tablespoons of the poaching liquid in a small saucepan; mix thoroughly and heat. Spoon over the oysters and place under a preheated broiler for 2 minutes.

Sprinkle with paprika and enjoy!

*Yield: 1 diet serving*
*Calories per serving: 334*

᳜§ *When you eat dinner in a restaurant, make sure to order a carbohydrate like potato, rice, or pasta. Skip the butter or sour cream.*

## *OYSTERS ROCK-A-BYE MENU PLAN*

*895 Calories (plus 200-calorie snack)*

Coffee, tea, or noncaloric beverages as desired

### BREAKFAST

½ cup unsweetened pineapple chunks
½ cup low-fat cottage cheese
1 slice raisin bread toast

(*Substitute:* Basic Breakfast 1)

### LUNCH

Green and Red Tuna
1 large green pepper, filled with
2 ounces water-packed tuna
½ tomato, chopped
1 scallion (optional)
1 tablespoon diet mayonnaise
1 1-ounce whole wheat bread pocket
1 cup skim milk

(*Substitute:* Basic Lunch 3)

### DINNER

1 diet serving Oysters Rock-a-Bye
½ serving any Super Salad
½ cup skim milk

## Eggs Benedict Arnold

We've named this dish after the most famous turncoat in American history not because there's anything traitorous about it, but because it's not what it appears to be.

Our eggs are covered with a *mock* hollandaise that is easy, delicious, and takes only minutes to prepare.

> 1 English muffin, split into two halves
> 1 thin slice boiled ham (½ ounce)
> 2 medium eggs
> ⅓ cup canned condensed cream of chicken soup
> 2 teaspoons tarragon vinegar
> 1 teaspoon prepared mustard
> 1 tablespoon plain low-fat yogurt
> Salt and freshly ground black pepper to taste
> Paprika

Scoop out as much of the center of each half muffin as possible without breaking through the bottom or edges. Toast.

Arrange one half slice of the ham in each half of the muffin. Break an egg over the ham and slide the halves onto a nonstick cookie sheet.

Bake in a preheated 350°F oven 5 minutes or until the whites have set.

Meanwhile, combine the soup, vinegar, and mustard in a small saucepan. Cook over moderate heat, stirring continually, until it begins to boil. Remove from the heat and stir in the yogurt completely.

Place the muffin halves on a serving plate and coat with the sauce. Sprinkle with salt, pepper, and paprika.

*Yield: 1 diet serving*
*Calories per serving: 343*

# EGGS BENEDICT ARNOLD MENU PLAN
*904 Calories (plus 200-calorie snack)*

Coffee, tea, or noncaloric beverages as desired

## BREAKFAST

⅓ cantaloupe *or* ½ grapefruit
½ cup low-fat cottage cheese
½ whole wheat English muffin

(*Substitute:* Basic Breakfast 1)

## LUNCH

Tostada with Cheese
  2 frozen corn tortillas, heated in a
    nonstick pan
  2 ounces Lite-line cheese, shredded
  ½ green pepper, chopped
  ½ medium tomato, chopped
  Salsa to taste
1 cup skim milk

(*Substitute:* Basic Lunch 3)

## DINNER

1 diet serving Eggs Benedict Arnold
½ serving any Super Salad
½ cup skim milk

# APPENDIX
## *Scientific Basis of the Carbohydrate Craver's Diet*

# INDEX

# APPENDIX

## *Scientific Basis of the Carbohydrate Craver's Diet*

People, rats, and many other animals have a specific hunger for carbohydrates — sweets and starches — that cannot be satisfied by eating any other kind of food. After a big steak dinner, you'll still be "hungry" for dessert. Three servings of salad at lunch will leave you unsatisfied because you haven't met your body's need for a carbohydrate-rich food. Between meals, when you get the urge to eat something, it will probably be a package of cookies, a candy bar, crackers, or ice cream.

Individuals have different degrees of carbohydrate hunger just as individuals need different amounts of sleep. In fact, most people who have no weight problem are unaware of carbohydrate hunger. They routinely satisfy it by eating starchy foods with their meals and by snacking on carbohydrate foods between meals. The overweight person is acutely aware of a craving for carbohydrates because sweets and starches are considered forbidden foods. And this craving is intensified on a high-protein–low-carbohydrate diet.

For years scientists have been aware of anecdotal evidence for carbohydrate hunger, but they assumed it was the same thing as the general need for food. They linked it with a drop in blood sugar levels and thought that the body was simply running out of energy. If you persisted in believing that carbohydrate hunger could be satisfied only with a sweet or starchy food, they said you had an overactive sweet tooth or blamed it on your emotions.

But they are wrong. My colleagues and I in our laboratory at the Department of Nutrition and Food Sciences at the Massachusetts Institute of Technology have shown that carbohydrate hunger actually exists. We have proved that this hunger comes not from an emotional need to eat sweet or starchy foods but from a specific metabolic need.

My interest in the existence of carbohydrate hunger goes back several years. About ten years ago, others at MIT had shown that the manufacture of a brain chemical, serotonin, is influenced by the amount of carbohydrate-rich foods an animal or a human eats. Serotonin, one of a class of brain chemicals known as neurotransmitters, is made from tryptophan, an amino acid. (Amino acids are the components of protein.) When carbohydrate foods are eaten, insulin is released into the blood. Insulin increases the amount of tryptophan that gets into the brain and, subsequently, the level and activity of serotonin. When enough serotonin is produced in the brain, it turns off the hunger for carbohydrate.

Although tryptophan is an amino acid found in protein, eating a protein-rich food such as meat or fish doesn't have the same effect. The reason is that tryptophan, in order to enter the brain, must compete with five other similarly shaped amino acids that all share the same system for being carried into the brain. The other amino acids in protein foods are more plentiful than tryptophan; tryptophan is the scarcest. So when you eat eggs or fish or meat, there are more of these competing amino acids than tryptophan being digested and sent into the blood. Therefore tryptophan has a much harder time getting into the brain. The result of eating a lot of protein is that the level of tryptophan in the brain does not increase and neither does the level of serotonin.

The way to increase the level of tryptophan in the brain is to eat starchy and sweet foods. When you eat carbohydrates, insulin is secreted into the blood, which at all times contains amino acids that are constantly moving between the blood and the cells. After insulin is secreted, these amino acids leave the blood very quickly and enter the muscle and other cells in the body. Tryptophan, however, is one amino acid that is not affected as much by insulin secretion. Tryptophan remains in the blood after the competition has disappeared. And with the competing amino acids out of the way, the tryptophan enters the brain easily, increases the amount of serotonin in the brain, and the serotonin sends out a signal that shuts off the carbohydrate hunger.

In other words, it takes carbohydrate foods to control carbohydrate hunger. But the carbohydrate food should be eaten alone, not with a food that contains protein or after a basically protein meal. If protein is combined with carbohydrate, the other amino acids from the protein will be competing with the tryptophan to get into the brain. Much less tryptophan will enter the brain than if you had eaten carbohydrate by itself.

This research on the carbohydrate connection between the diet and the brain stimulated our search for a specific carbohydrate hunger. We began some studies on rats in our laboratory and discovered that the rats did, indeed, have a specific hunger for carbohydrates. When they were allowed to control the amount they ate, they ate a constant proportion every day. It didn't matter whether the carbohydrate was a sweet or a starch: they ate the same amount.

We also found that after their carbohydrate hunger was satisfied, the rats found something else to eat. In one experiment we fed half our rats six calories' worth of sugary homemade mints and the other half six calories' worth of peanut butter, which is mostly fat. Then we gave both sets of rats a choice of two foods, one containing a lot of carbohydrate, the other very little. The mint-fed rats were obviously satisfied with the sugar in their candy because they chose the low-carbohydrate food. The rats that had been fed peanut butter, on the other hand, primarily chose the high-carbohydrate food.

What this meant was not only that a carbohydrate hunger exists, but that when it is satisfied, it goes away. We learned that serotonin is involved in turning off this hunger by giving rats a drug that increased the activity of this brain chemical. The rats treated with the drug ate much less carbohydrate (but not protein) than rats given an inert placebo. It seemed to us that a cycle occurs when carbohydrates are eaten. The sweet or starchy food causes insulin to be secreted, causing tryptophan to enter the brain easily and make serotonin. Serotonin then sends out a signal saying "Stop eating carbohydrates."

These results suggested the possibility of devising a diet that would satisfy the Carbohydrate Craver's need for carbohydrate. Such a diet would promote weight loss without causing an insatiable longing for sweet and starchy foods. It would be a low-calorie diet that contained enough carbohydrates at and between meals to cause serotonin to shut off the carbohydrate hunger. But first we wanted to make sure that a carbohydrate hunger really exists in humans.

We next turned our attention to people, specifically overweight people, who claimed to overeat only carbohydrate foods. Our human volunteers confirmed what we had already found out with our laboratory rats: people, too, have a distinct hunger for carbohydrates, and serotonin is involved in its regulation.

But if it is true, as our research showed, that people and rats have a need for carbohydrates, why can't the human Carbohydrate Craver be more like the rat and satisfy the craving with only small amounts of carbohydrates?

The first reason is that humans who try to lose weight choose diets that deprive them of the carbohydrates their bodies need. The second is that when Carbohydrate Cravers do eat carbohydrates, they feel guilty. Both these factors make people overeat.

When you go on a diet that eliminates all but the small amounts of carbohydrates found in fruit and vegetables, your body temporarily loses its ability to control its carbohydrate hunger. We found that when our rats were deprived of carbohydrates for a few weeks, they responded by binging — eating much more carbohydrate than normal — because the signal from the brain that says "Stop, you've had enough" was not produced soon enough. The delay may occur because a smaller-than-usual amount of insulin is secreted when carbohydrates have not been consumed for several days. That's why you aren't satisfied with eating a small amount of carbohydrate after you go off one of those high-protein–low-carbohydrate diets. You, like the rats, have to eat a lot of carbohydrate to produce enough serotonin to shut off your carbohydrate hunger.

The other thing that happens is that your guilt and anxiety over eating these "fattening" foods prevent you from realizing that your carbohydrate hunger is finally satisfied. People who are able to control their carbohydrate hunger with normal amounts of carbohydrates are aware of feeling better after snacking or eating a high-carbohydrate meal.

# Index

&#8766; Traveling and don't know what to eat for breakfast? Order grapefruit juice or melon, boiled or poached eggs, and unbuttered whole wheat toast. This low-fat meal supplies plenty of nutrients for the day ahead with relatively few calories.

&#8766; Never weigh yourself one or two days after a big or bulky meal. The scale will register the weight of any water you may retain until the food is totally assimilated.

&#8766; Are you a member of the clean-plate club? Make sure you weigh or measure what you put on that plate so you don't clean up excess calories.

&#8766; A hidden leftover will not be nibbled. Remember: out of sight, out of mouth.

&#8766; Going to a catered dinner? Eat something before you go, decline anything with mysterious, breaded, sauced, cheesed, or buttered ingredients. Don't allow dessert to be put in front of you. After all, you're going for the company, not for the food.

*⋴§ If you feel guilty about throwing out leftovers because so many people in the world are hungry, throw them out anyway and contribute your money or time to charities that feed the hungry.*

*⋴§ If you have extra time at night or over a weekend, cook for a few days and store the food in the refrigerator or freezer. It's like having extra money in the bank.*

*⋴§ Find it hard to exercise alone? Consider joining a Y or exercise group. Or go on bird-watching expeditions or photography walks.*

*⋴§ Avoid nibbling while preparing food by cooking as much as possible in the morning, as you're making breakfast. Foods that tempt you at 5 P.M. tend to be most unappealing at 7 A.M.*

*⋴§ Talk on the phone a lot? Try pacing, doing knee bends, or even slow sit-ups. Just try not to grunt into the phone.*